The Raintree Illustrated
Science Encyclopedia

9 $\frac{haw}{int}$

The Raintree Illustrated
SCIENCE
ENCYCLOPEDIA

Raintree Publishers Limited
Milwaukee • Toronto • Melbourne • London

Library of Congress Number: 78-12093

1 2 3 4 5 6 7 8 9 0 83 82 81 80 79

Printed in the United States of America.

Library of Congress Cataloging in Publication Data

Main entry under title:

The Raintree illustrated science encyclopedia.

 Includes index.
 SUMMARY: An encyclopedia of principles, concepts, and
people in the various fields of science and technology.
 1. Science — Dictionaries, Juvenile. [1. Science —
Dictionaries]
Q121.R34   503   78-12093

ISBN 0-8172-1225-6 (set) trade
ISBN 0-8172-1234-5 (volume 9)

ISBN 0-8172-1202-7 (set) lib. bdg.
ISBN 0-8172-1211-6 (volume 9)

PUBLISHER:
Richard W. Weening

**ASSOCIATE PUBLISHER
AND PROJECT MANAGER:**
Russell Bennett

EDITORS:
Patricia Daniels
Patricia Krapesh-Wolz
Herta S. Breiter
James I. Clark
Richard Hagle
Georgianne Heymann

ART DIRECTOR:
Jane Palecek

PRODUCTION MANAGER:
Conrad J. Charles

MANAGING EDITOR:
George C. Kohn (G.C.K.)

EDITORS:
Jerome J. Ackerman (J.J.A.)
John Andrewartha (J.A.)
Anthony J. Castagno (A.J.C.)
Joseph M. Castagno (J.M.C.)
Martin Elliott (M.E.)
Stephen R. Gephard (S.R.G.)
Hope Gilbert (H.G.)
Christine Madsen (C.M.)
William R. Parker (W.R.P.)
David M. H. Williams (D.M.H.W.)

ASSOCIATE EDITORS:
Sheila A. Barnett (S.A.B.)
George M. Bray III (G.M.B.)
Paul G. Cheatham (P.G.C.)
Richard H. Hauck (R.H.H.)

EDITORIAL ASSISTANT:
Jean Soja

BIBLIOGRAPHER:
Mary Jane Anderson
Executive Secretary,
Asociation for Library Services to Children,
American Library Association

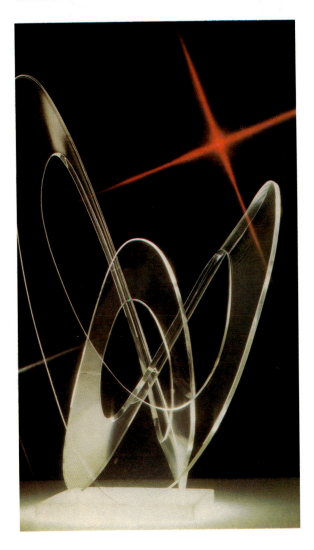

USING THE RAINTREE ILLUSTRATED
SCIENCE ENCYCLOPEDIA

You are living in a world in which science, technology, and nature are very important. You see something about science almost every day. It might be on television, in the newspaper, in a book at school, or in some other place. Often you want more information about what you see. *The Raintree Illustrated Science Encyclopedia* will help you find what you want to know. The Raintree encyclopedia has information on many science subjects. You may want to find out about mathematics, biology, agriculture, computer science, lasers, or rockets, for example. They are all in *The Raintree Illustrated Science Encyclopedia*. And there are many, many other subjects.

There are twenty volumes in the encyclopedia. The articles, which are called entries, are in alphabetical order. On the front of each volume, next to the volume number, are some letters. The letters above the line are the first three letters of the first entry in that volume. The letters below the line are the first three letters of the last entry in that volume. In Volume 1, for example, you see that the first entry begins with **aar** and that the last entry begins with **arg**. Using the letters makes it easy to find the volume you need.

At the back of each volume, there are interesting projects you can do on your own. The projects are fun to do, and they illustrate important science principles.

In Volume 20, there are two special features — an index and a bibliography. They are described in Volume 20.

Main Entries. The titles of the main entries in *The Raintree Illustrated Science Encyclopedia* are printed in capital letters. They look like this: **CAMERA**.

The titles of some of the longer or more important entries are printed in larger capital letters.

At the beginning of each entry, you will see a phonetic pronunciation of the entry title. On page viii, there is a pronunciation key. Use it the same way you use your dictionary key.

At the end of each entry, there are two sets of initials. They look like this: S.R.G./W.R.S. The first set belongs to the person who wrote the entry. The second set belongs to the special consultant who checked the entry for accuracy. Pages v and vi give you the names of all these people. Throughout the Raintree encyclopedia, measurements are given in both the metric and English systems.

Cross-References. Sometimes a subject has two names. The Raintree encyclopedia usually puts the information with the more common name. But in case you look up the less common name, there will be a cross-reference to tell you where to find the information. Suppose you wanted to look up something about the metric temperature scale. This scale is usually called the Celsius Scale. Sometimes, however, it is called the Centigrade Scale. The Raintree encyclopedia has the entry Celsius Scale. But if you had looked up Centigrade Scale, you would have found this: **CENTIGRADE SCALE** *See* CELSIUS SCALE. This kind of cross-reference tells you where to find the information you need.

There is another kind of cross-reference in the Raintree encyclopedia. It looks like this *See* **CLOUD** or like this *See also* **ELECTRICITY**. These cross-references tell you where to find other helpful information on the subject you are reading about.

Projects. At the end of some entries, you will see this symbol ◣. That tells you that there is a project on that entry at the back of the volume.

Illustrations. There are thousands of photos, charts, diagrams, and tables in the Raintree encyclopedia. They will help you better understand the entries you read. A caption describes each picture. Many of the pictures also have labels that point out important parts.

Index. The index lists every main entry by volume and page number. In addition, many subjects that are not main entries are also listed in the index.

Bibliography. In Volume 20, there is also a bibliography. The books in this list are on the same general subjects covered in the Raintree encyclopedia.

The Raintree Illustrated Science Encyclopedia was designed especially for you, the young reader. It is a source of knowledge for the world of science, technology, and nature. Enjoy it.

PRONUNCIATION GUIDE

These symbols have the same sound as the
darker letters in the sample words.

ə	balloon, ago	ō	cone, know
ər	learn, further	ȯ	all, saw
a	map, have	ȯi	boy, boil
ā	day, made	p	part, scrap
ä	father, car	r	root, tire
aù	now, loud	s	so, press
b	ball, rib	sh	shoot, machine
ch	choose, nature	t	to, stand
d	did, add	th	thin, death
e	bell, get	<u>th</u>	then, <u>th</u>is
ē	sweet, easy	ü	pool, lose
f	fan, soft	ù	put, book
g	good, big	v	view, give
h	hurt, ahead	w	wood, glowing
i	rip, ill	y	yes, year
ī	side, sky	z	zero, raise
j	join, germ	zh	leisure, vision
k	king, ask		
l	let, cool		
m	man, same	′	strong accent
n	no, turn	′	weak accent

HAWTHORN (hồ' thồrn) The hawthorn is any of several species of small deciduous trees or shrubs belonging to the genus *Crataegus* of the rose family. The stems have many thorns, and alternate, simple, toothed or lobed leaves. The flowers usually grow in clusters at the ends of the stems. They have five petals and may be white, red, or pink. The fruits, or haws, are applelike and may be red, orange, blue, or black.

The English hawthorn (*Crataegus oxyacantha*) is frequently grown in hedges. It blossoms in May and produces red haws. Its leaves change colors to red or yellow before dropping off in the fall. The English hawthorn is also called mayhaw, red haw, or scarlet haw.

The downy hawthorn (*Crataegus mollis*) is a common United States species. It has white flowers and orange haws. *See also* ROSE FAMILY.   A.J.C./M.H.S.

Tiny hearing aids are in these eye glasses.

HEARING AID (hir′ ing ād) A hearing aid is an electronic device that improves a per-son's ability to hear. Many deaf and hard-of-hearing persons depend upon this device.

There are two general types of hearing aids: air-conduction aids and bone-conduction aids. The air-conduction aid simplifies sound and brings it directly to the ear. Some persons, however, cannot use this type of hearing aid because they cannot receive sound waves through the inner and outer ear. These people use bone-conduction aids that bring sound waves to the bony parts of the head behind the ear. The bone transmits the vibrations to the auditory nerves of the cochlea. (*See* EAR.) Hearing becomes possible when these nerves are stimulated.

Hearing aids in use today are basically electronic devices that resemble miniature telephones. They consist of a microphone, an amplifier, receiver, and a battery power supply. The receiver fits in the ear, in the case of the air-conduction type, and behind the ear, for the bone-conduction variety. Hearing aids are compact and easy to carry and conceal. Usually the only part visible to the public is the receiver and the wire attached to it. Newly-developed aids have even eliminated the wire. One type of hearing aid is completely contained within the frame of a pair of glasses. Hearing aids can be adjusted to a wide range of frequencies and tones.

Air-conduction aids and bone-conduction aids have been used for many years. The principle of bone-conduction was known in the 1600s. The ear trumpet, a simple hornlike device, was used to improve hearing even earlier. In the late 1700s, the audiphone was invented. It was a cardboard, or celluloid, device shaped like a fan. Users held the edge between their teeth, and bent the fan towards the sound. The sound vibrations traveled from the teeth, to the jawbone, the skull, and to the auditory nerves.

In 1872, Alexander Graham Bell began experimenting with electric devices that would help deaf children to hear. Although he never invented a hearing aid, his work did lead to the development of the telephone. The first electronic hearing aid was developed around 1900. It was bulky and inconvenient to use. The vacuum tube aid was the next type to come along. It consisted of a crystal microphone, a vacuum tube amplifier, and batteries. In 1953, the electronic transistor hearing aid was introduced. It completely replaced the vacuum tube aid because it was much smaller and less expensive to operate. This is the type in use today. W.R.P./L.L.R.

HEART (härt) The heart is a powerful pump that drives the blood around the body. The human heart is about the size of a closed fist. It lies in the chest between the two lungs. It is not in the center of the chest. Instead, it lies just a little to the left side of the body. The heart is a hollow organ divided into four chambers. The walls of these four chambers are made of powerful muscle. When the mus-

cle in the walls shortens, or contracts, it makes the chambers smaller. This squeezes the blood out of the heart into blood vessels called arteries. (*See* ARTERY.) In the human heart, a wall of muscle separates completely the right and left sides. Blood in the two sides cannot mix. The two sides of the heart work together. They pump blood through the two chambers at the same time. The right side pumps its blood to the lungs. The left side pumps its blood to all other parts of the body.

The two lower chambers of the heart are called ventricles. The left ventricle has very thick walls of muscle. It is the most powerful pumping chamber of the heart. It pumps blood into a large blood vessel called the aorta. (*See* AORTA.) The aorta branches out into many smaller arteries. The arteries carry blood that is rich in oxygen to all parts of the body. The left ventricle releases its blood into the arteries in rapid jets or squirts. These

Deoxygenated blood (dark red) returns to the heart through the superior and inferior vena cavas. The right ventricle pumps this blood to the lungs, where it picks up oxygen (light red) and returns to the left atrium. From the left ventricle, it is pumped through the aorta to the body.

Four heart chambers are illustrated below. A fish has two chambers. An amphibian has three chambers with two atria and an undivided ventricle. A reptile has four chambers, but the ventricles are not completely divided. A bird or a mammal has four chambers with completely divided ventricles.

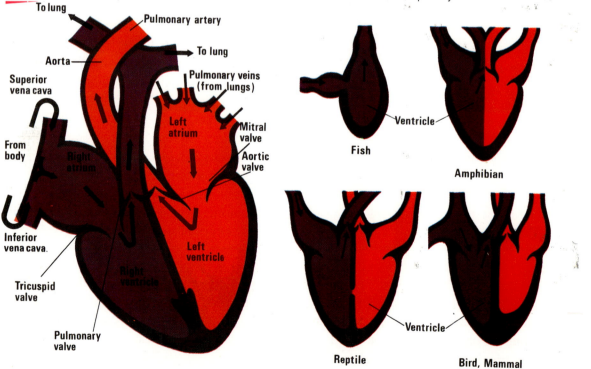

squirts of blood make the pulse that we can feel in some blood vessels just beneath the skin. (*See* PULSE.) As the blood travels around the body, it loses its oxygen and picks up a waste chemical called carbon dioxide. The blood then has to be returned to the right side of the heart. From there, it can be pumped to the lungs. Blood travels back to the heart through blood vessels called veins. (*See* VEIN.) The veins empty their blood into two large vessels called venae cavae. (*See* VENA CAVA.) The venae cavae empty blood into an upper chamber of the heart called the right atrium (also called the right auricle). The right atrium contracts and squeezes blood into the right ventricle. The right ventricle forces its blood into a blood vessel called the pulmonary artery. The pulmonary artery takes blood to the lungs. In the lungs, the blood loses its carbon dioxide. This is breathed out. At the same time, the blood takes up more oxygen. When the blood is rich in oxygen, it is carried to the left side of the heart. It is carried in a blood vessel called the pulmonary vein. The pulmonary vein empties its blood into the left atrium (also called the left auricle). The blood then passes into the left ventricle. It can now start its long journey around the body again. There are flaps, or valves, in the heart that keep the blood from flowing backward. The blood has to keep flowing in one direction only. There are valves between the atria (plural of atrium) and ventricles. There are also valves at the exit from each ventricle.

The heart beats automatically. It does not need to be controlled by the brain. Sometimes the heart gets messages that make it change the speed of its beat. It can go faster or slower. These messages can come from special nerve signals. They can also come from special chemicals carried in the blood. (*See* HORMONE.) The continuous and regular beating of the heart is controlled by the pacemaker. The pacemaker lies between the two atria. It is in a small group of muscle cells that send out regular electrical signals. These signals make the atria get smaller, or contract. When these signals reach the ventricles lower down, those ventricles contract as well. The atria always contract just before the ventricles. The heartbeat is carefully timed and controlled. The contraction of the chambers is called the systole. The short period of rest that follows is called the diastole. The systole and diastole repeat alternately throughout the life of a person. In a healthy adult, the heart beats about 70 times a minute. During exercise or very heavy work, the heart may beat more than 140 times a minute. *See also* HEART DISEASES.

J.A./J.J.F.

HEART DISEASE (härt′ diz ēz′) The heart is the hardest-working organ in the body. We rely on it to work efficiently every moment of every day. Any disorder that stops it pumping properly is a threat to life. Heart disease is very common. More people are killed every year in the U.S. by heart disease than by any other disease. There are many kinds of heart disease.

Congenital disease   A congenital disease is one that a person is born with. Most babies are born with perfect hearts. But in about one in every two hundred babies, something goes wrong. Sometimes a valve grows with the wrong shape. It may be too tight, or fail to close properly. Sometimes a gap is left in the wall, or septum, between the two sides of the heart. This is often called a "septal defect." Sometimes the blood vessels grow to join the wrong chambers of the heart.

When a baby's heart is badly formed, it cannot work efficiently. The blood does not receive enough oxygen. The baby becomes breathless. The blood cannot get rid of carbon dioxide through the lungs. It becomes purplish, and the baby's skin looks blue. Fortunately, it is now possible to save the lives of many "blue babies." Surgeons are often able to operate on the heart and fix congenital faults.

Rheumatic disease The disease called rheumatic fever may cause harm to the heart. The disease usually follows a sore throat caused by bacteria called streptococci. The tissues of the heart become inflamed. If it is badly affected, the heart fails. Usually, however, it recovers. The results of the damage are seen only years later. The valves of the heart are left with scars. They cannot work properly. This puts a strain on the heart. Eventually it may fail. The effects of the rheumatic fever may take up to twenty or thirty years to show.

Today doctors can operate on the heart and replace faulty valves. Artificial valves are made of metal and plastics. This kind of operation saves many lives every year. There are many other diseases that can cause damage to the muscle and lining of the heart.

Coronary disease The arteries that supply blood to the heart itself are called the coronary arteries. They are very important. They give the heart muscle the oxygen it needs to carry on working. If the coronary arteries become blocked, parts of the heart muscle die. The patient has a "heart attack," which can be fatal. Or the heart may be so damaged that the patient is left as an invalid.

The blockage of the coronary arteries is usually caused by clots of blood. A clot of blood is called a thrombus. When a clot forms in a coronary artery, this is called coronary thrombosis. That is the correct name for a heart attack.

In normal arteries, blood does not form clots. But in coronary disease, the walls of the arteries are not normal. They become lumpy, rough, and narrow. The lumps are called atheroma. In atheroma, a blood clot may suddenly form inside an artery. It may cause thrombosis.

Atheroma are thought to be due to too much of certain fatty substances in the blood. A substance called cholesterol is usually blamed. Many people follow diets that cut down on cholesterol in the blood. However, many other things are also blamed for heart disease. Lack of exercise, being overweight, and smoking are all bad for the heart. *See also* HEART.   D.M.H.W./J.J.F.

HEARTWOOD (härt′ wŭd) Heartwood is the central part of a tree trunk. It is made up of dead, non-functioning cells which contain tannin and other chemicals. (*See* TANNING.) These chemicals make the heartwood appear darker than the surrounding sapwood. Sapwood is softer than heartwood, and is made up of living cells.

Heartwood is very strong and is resistant to decay. Each year, one or more layers of sapwood cells are converted into heartwood. Heartwood is sometimes called duramen.
                A.J.C./M.H.S.

HEAT

All matter contains heat (hēt). Heat is a form of energy. The heat energy present in any object is connected with its temperature. If the object gains heat energy, its temperature rises. If it loses heat energy, its temperature falls. There is an important difference between heat and temperature. The amount of heat energy depends on the amount of matter present. For example, a heated swimming pool contains much more heat than a pan of boiling water, even though the pan has a higher temperature. This is because there is much more water in the swimming pool than in the pan.

All matter is made up of tiny particles called atoms. These atoms are continually moving. Movement is a form of energy. It is called kinetic energy. The heat energy in matter is the total kinetic energy of all its atoms. The temperature depends on how fast the atoms are moving.

Temperature is measured by a thermome-

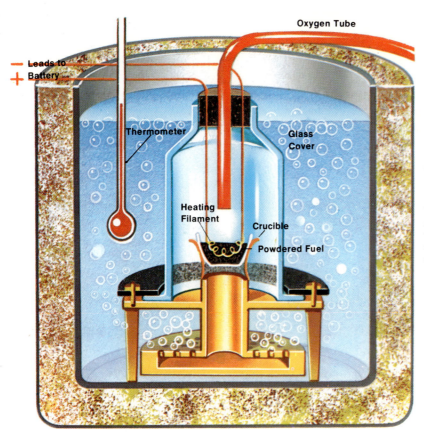

Oxygen Tube

Leads to Battery

Thermometer

Glass Cover

Heating Filament

Crucible

Powdered Fuel

Diagram of a calorimeter, a device used to measure the caloric value of different fuels. A measured amount of a powdered fuel is put in the crucible inside the glass cover and set on fire by the electric filament. A stream of oxygen keeps the fuel burning. The heat given off raises the temperature of a measured amount of water surrounding the glass cover. A thermometer measures the temperature change.

ter in units of degrees Celsius or Fahrenheit. Heat energy is measured in joules or calories. It is measured by an instrument called a calorimeter.

As the temperature of a substance drops, its atoms move more slowly. Eventually, a point could be reached where the atoms would stop moving altogether. The temperature at this point is called absolute zero. At absolute zero, the substance has no heat energy at all. In fact, although scientists have cooled substances to within a fraction of a degree of absolute zero, no substance can be cooled down to absolute zero. Matter always contains some heat energy.

Heat has two common effects on a body. One is that it can cause bodies to change their states. For example, it can turn a solid into a liquid, such as ice into water. Or it can turn a liquid into a gas, such as water into steam. In a solid, the atoms are kept at fixed points by forces acting between the atoms. The atoms can only move a short distance about their fixed points. They cannot move through the whole of the solid, unlike the atoms in liquids and gases. As the temperature rises, the atoms move further away from their fixed points. Eventually, they can move so far away that the structure of the solid breaks down and becomes a liquid.

In a liquid, the forces between the atoms still have some effect. That is why a liquid has a definite volume. But the atoms are not held to any one place. They can move freely throughout the liquid. Then, as the heat increases, the liquid turns into a gas. The atoms are able to move too fast for the forces between them to have much effect.

At even higher temperatures, there is another state of matter. It is called a plasma. In a plasma, the atoms lose some, or perhaps all, of their electrons. A plasma contains free-moving ions and electrons.

Another effect of heat is that it causes substances to expand. When an atom moves faster, it takes up more room. Therefore, the hotter the substance, the larger its volume. Solids and liquids expand only a very little with temperature. Gases expand much more.

Sources of heat Many chemical reactions produce heat. These reactions are called exothermic reactions. An example of an exothermic reaction is the burning of a fuel. When a fuel burns, it combines with the oxygen in the air. This reaction gives off a large amount of heat. Another exothermic reaction is rusting. Rusting only produces a very small amount of heat. The amount is too small for us to notice.

Heat is a form of energy and one form of energy can be converted into another form. Heat can be produced from several different forms of energy. For example, heat can be produced by friction. When two objects are rubbed together, energy is needed to overcome the friction between them. This energy is converted into heat and the objects become warm. Our most important source of heat is the sun. These reactions produce huge amounts of heat.

Movement of heat Heat can travel by three different methods: conduction, convection, and radiation. In conduction, the heat is transferred from one atom to another. In this way, heat moves through a substance. Conduction occurs in solids and in liquids. It also occurs in gases to a small extent. Suppose you put a metal cooking pot over a fire. The handle of the pot becomes hot, even though it is not in the fire. The atoms near the fire become hot and start to move quickly. They collide with atoms nearby and pass on some of their energy. The energy is slowly transmitted further away from the fire. In this way, the whole of the pot becomes hot. Some solids, such as plastics, do not transmit much heat. They are called insulators. (*See* INSULATION.) Other substances, such as metals, transmit

most of their heat. They are called conductors. (*See* CONDUCTION.)

In convection, heated matter moves from one point to another. Convection can occur in both liquids and gases. It does not occur in solids. The air around a fire becomes heated. As it becomes heated, it expands. The air becomes lighter and rises. This causes convection currents in the air. Winds and currents in the sea are partly caused by convection currents. They are caused by one part of the atmosphere or the sea being hotter than another part.

Heat can also travel without matter being present. It travels in the form of infrared radiation. This is how the heat from the sun reaches us through space. When infrared radiation hits an object, it heats it up. Infrared radiation is given off by the atoms and molecules of all hot objects.

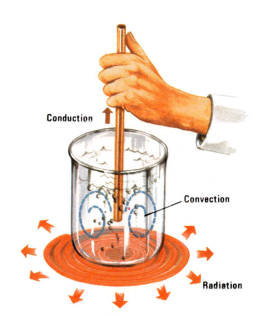

Heat travels by radiation, convection, and conduction as shown here.

History of heat Before 1800, scientists thought of heat as a fluid. They called the fluid "caloric." Then a number of scientists demonstrated a connection between heat and energy. The most important of these scientists was a British physicist, James Joule. He showed that a falling weight can heat water. He concluded that some of the kinetic energy of the weight was converted into heat.

At the same time, John Dalton, British chemist, put forward his atomic theory. His theory said that all matter is made up of atoms. Scientists soon combined these two theories and concluded that heat is caused by the motion of atoms. *See also* THERMODYNAMICS. M.E./J.D.

HEATH FAMILY The heath (hēth) family, Ericaceae, contains nearly 2,500 plants. Most are shrubs and herbs. Many are evergreens. These plants are found in temperate climates and in high elevations of the tropics. They grow best in sandy, acidic soil. Well-known members of the heath family include the rhododendron, mountain laurel, azalea, blueberry, and cranberry. *See also* EVERGREEN; LAUREL. S.R.G./M.H.S.

The Heath Family included about 500 members of the genus *Erica*. *Erica cinerea* is shown here.

HEAT SHIELD (hēt shēld) A heat shield is a plastic and asbestos coating, or metal structure, on a rocket nose cone, or on a spacecraft. It protects the astronauts and instruments from the intense heat produced during high-speed flights through the atmosphere. Heating occurs when a spacecraft leaves outer space and reenters earth's atmosphere at high speeds. Molecules of air generate heat by friction against the surface of the spacecraft. There is no air in outer space to create this problem. The greater the spacecraft's speed of reentry, the more intense the heat.

Common types of heat shields are ablative shields, and heat sinks. Ablative shields use up the heat by melting and vaporizing. The air stream carries away the hot gas vapors and the molten particles. Heat sinks simply absorb great amounts of heat, and thus prevent it from reaching the occupants and instruments. Fast-flying airplanes use this method. *See also* SPACE TRAVEL. W.R.P./J.vP.

Machining of an Apollo spacecraft heat shield, a device that protects the craft from air friction.

HEAT TREATMENT (hēt′ trēt′ mənt) In industry, metals are often heated and then cooled. This often makes them stronger or harder. The general term for this is heat treatment. There are a number of different methods of heat treatment. One is called annealing. The metal is heated to above a particular temperature. This temperature is called the critical temperature. It varies for different metals. Above this temperature, the metal loses any stresses that it may have inside it. These stresses can greatly weaken the metal. The metal is kept above this temperature for a while and then slowly cooled. The cooling is done in a furnace, so that it can be controlled. Annealing makes the metal softer. It can then be more easily shaped or drawn out into wire. Annealing is also carried out on glass.

Another method of heat treatment is called hardening. The metal is heated to above its critical temperature. Then it is cooled very quickly by dipping it into water or oil. This makes the metal very hard, but also very brittle. Hardening is usually followed by another process called tempering. The metal is again heated, but only to below its critical temperature this time. Then it is slowly cooled. This reduces the brittleness, but also makes the metal less hard.   M.E./A.D.

HEAVY ELEMENT (hev′ ē el′ ə mənt) Heavy element is a term commonly used in nuclear physics to describe elements with high atomic numbers, such as uranium (atomic number 92) and plutonium (94). If one element is said to be heavier than another, this often indicates that it has a higher atomic number. *See also* NUCLEAR PHYSICS.

   J.J.A./J.R.W.

HEAVY WATER (hev′ ē wȯt′ ər) Water molecules each contain two atoms of hydrogen and one of oxygen. This is written H_2O. Hydrogen has an isotope called deuterium. (*See* ISOTOPE.) Deuterium has the same chemical properties as hydrogen and can replace hydrogen in its compounds. If deuterium replaces the hydrogen in water,

then heavy water is formed. Heavy water is also known as deuterium oxide and its formula is D_2O. Heavy water occurs naturally in small amounts. About one part in 4,500 of ordinary water is heavy water.

Deuterium is heavier than ordinary hydrogen. This makes heavy water heavier than ordinary water. One cubic centimeter of water weighs one gram at 20°C [68°F]. The same volume of heavy water weighs 1.1 grams at 20°C. Its freezing and boiling points are also slightly different. Water freezes at 0°C [32°F] and boils at 100°C [212°F]. Heavy water freezes at 3.8°C [38.8°F] and boils at 101.4°C [214.5°F].

If an electric current is passed through water, hydrogen and oxygen gases are given off. This is called electroylsis. (*See* ELECTROLYSIS.) If the water contains some deuterium, then it too is given off. But it is given off more slowly than ordinary hydrogen. As the current flows, the water becomes richer in heavy water. This is how heavy water is obtained from ordinary water. Heavy water is sometimes used in nuclear reactors to control the spread of the reaction. It is also used to keep the reactor cool.

   M.E./S.R.W.

HEISENBERG, WERNER (1901–1976) Werner Heisenberg (hī′ zən bərg) was a German atomic physicist. He was awarded the Nobel Prize for Physics in 1932 for his work on quantum mechanics (*See* QUANTUM THEORY.) He was director of the Max Planck Institute for Physics in Berlin from 1942 to 1945. He is famous for his work on the uncertainty principle. (*See* UNCERTAINTY PRINCIPLE.)   C.M./D.G.F.

HELICOPTER (hel′ ə käp′ tər) A helicopter is an aircraft that has a number of horizontal blades. These blades together are called

Facing right: some helicopters have two main rotors, which spin in opposite directions.

A helicopter flies by changing the pitch of its main rotor blades. A sharp pitch sends the plane up. A medium pitch lets it hover. Changing pitch on the back blade sends the ship forward, or backward.

the rotor. They rotate very fast and allow the helicopter to fly in any direction through the air. The rotor takes the place of both the wings and propellers of a regular fixed-wing aircraft. Helicopters can fly straight up or down and do not need a runway. They can also fly forwards, backwards, or sideways. Or they can hover in one position. This is all done by altering the pitch of the blades. The pitch is the angle at which the blades are set. If the blades lie flat, the helicopter moves downward. If they are pitched up, then the helicopter moves upward. By tilting the rotor, the helicopter can be steered in the desired direction.

Some helicopters also have a small, vertical rotor at the back. This helps to stabilize the helicopter. As the main rotor rotates, its motor tends to cause the helicopter to rotate in the opposite direction. The tail rotor works against the rotation and prevents it from happening. The tail rotor also allows the helicopter to change direction. Some large helicopters have two, or even four, main rotors and no tail rotors. These rotors spin in opposite directions. This cancels out the twisting effect of each rotor. Therefore, no tail rotor is needed. M.E./J.vP.

HELIOGRAPHY (hē lē äg′ rə fē) The word heliography is derived from the Greek word *helios*, meaning sun. During the 1700s,

the branch of astronomy concerning the sun was called heliography. In the early 1800s, heliography meant photography. During the late 1800s, heliography was a method of sending messages by the reflection of sunlight. This was done by an instrument called a heliograph. The heliograph used mirrors to reflect the sunlight. The messages were sent in flashes, representing Morse code symbols. These flashes could be seen 48 km [30 mi] away with the naked eye.

Today, meteorologists use an instrument, also called a heliograph, to measure the intensity of the sun, and to detect dust and other particles in the air. This heliograph is used to study and predict air pollution. J.M.C./C.R.

HELIUM (hē′ lē əm) Helium (He) is a colorless, gaseous element. It is the second lightest gas after hydrogen. The atomic number of helium is 2 and its atomic weight is 4.0026. Helium boils at −268.9°C [−452°F]. This is the lowest boiling point of any element. Unlike every other element, helium does not turn into a solid by cooling alone. It has to be pressurized as well. It solidifies at −269.7°C [−453.5°F] and under a pressure 103 times that of the atomosphere. Helium is one of the noble gases and is very unreactive.

Helium was first discovered in 1868 by the British chemist Sir Joseph Lockyer and the

French chemist Pierre Janssen. They used an instrument called a spectroscope to discover helium in the sun. Helium was not found on earth until 1895. Then, the British chemist Sir William Ramsay discovered helium in the mineral clevite. Helium is named after the Greek work for sun, *helios*.

Several radioactive elements give off helium when they decay. That is why it occurs in certain minerals. Helium can also be obtained from natural gas. The gas wells in Colorado and Texas contain as much as 8% helium. Helium is also formed during thermonuclear fusion of hydrogen. This is how the sun and other stars obtain their energy. Stars contain vast amounts of helium. For this reason, helium is the second most abundant element in the universe after hydrogen.

Since helium is so light, it is used for filling balloons. Hydrogen was once used for this but hydrogen is a dangerous gas because it burns explosively in air. Helium is much safer to use because it is so unreactive. Helium is also used in the gas breathed in by deep-sea divers. They used to breathe ordinary air, which contains nitrogen, but this is dangerous. Deep down in the sea, the pressure is very great. This causes the nitrogen in the air to dissolve in the blood. In the past, when the divers surfaced, the pressure quickly returned to normal. This caused the nitrogen to bubble quickly out of the blood. This is called the bends and can be very painful and can even kill the diver. Today, divers breathe a mixture of oxygen and helium. Helium does not easily dissolve in the blood and so is much safer to use. Breathing helium makes divers speak with a high, squeaky voice. This is because sound travels three times as fast in helium as it does in air. This raises the pitch of a sound.

Like all gases, helium can be liquefied. There are two kinds of liquid helium, helium I and helium II. Helium I changes into helium II below −271°C [−456°F]. Helium I is a normal liquid but helium II is very strange. It is called a superfluid. If helium II is placed in a container, it creeps up the sides. Eventually it flows over the top and down the outside of the container. This happens because a superfluid has almost no viscosity. M.E./J.R.W.

Although rare on earth, helium is, after hydrogen, the most abundant element in the universe. Helium is produced in the sun and other stars as a result of the nuclear fusion of hydrogen. These reactions produce great heat.

HELLBENDER (hel′ ben′ dər) The hellbender is a large salamander that belongs to the family Cryptobranchidae. They are large amphibians with a long, fat, black body, large head, and four short legs. Hellbenders may reach lengths of 51 cm [20 in]. They live in warm, slow-moving streams. Although many people think they are poisonous, hellbenders are quite harmless.

Although they have lungs, hellbenders do not use them to breathe. Instead, the air stored is used to float the animal. Breathing is done through the skin, especially along the long flap of skin that extends along each side of the animal.

There are two subspecies of hellbenders in North America. The hellbender is found in east-central United States. The Ozark hellbender is found only in the streams of the Ozark Mountains in southern Missouri and northern Arkansas. *See* AMPHIBIAN; SALAMANDER. S.R.G./R.L.L.

HELMHOLTZ, HERMANN (1821–1894)

Hermann Helmholtz (helm' hòltz) was a German scientist. He was first a surgeon and then a physicist. He made many discoveries connected with vision and hearing. He studied color vision and also invented the opthalmoscope. He wrote a book about how the ear works.

As a physicist, Helmholtz also studied sound, electricity, and light. His work helped to develop the theory of the conservation of energy. His work on electromagnetism led to the electromagnetic theory of light. *See also* ACCOMMODATION; CONSERVATION OF ENERGY.

C.M./D.G.F.

HEMATITE (hē' mə tīt') Hematite (Fe_2O_3)
is an important iron ore. It is ferric oxide, a compound of iron and oxygen. Hematite can be black, brownish red, or dark red. A fresh scratch on hematite is blood red. The word ''hematite'' means bloodlike. The ore occurs in various forms, such as shiny crystals, grainy rock, and loose, earthy material. One interesting variety is kidney ore. It is so called because it is shaped in round masses that look

Hematite, one of the main iron ores, is so named because its color is blood-red. Shown here is the variety of hematite known as kidney ore, which looks like kidneys.

like kidneys. One form of hematite called red ocher is used to color paint.

Large amounts of hematite occur in Canada, Brazil, China, and Britain. The United States has the world's largest and most productive hematite mines around Lake Superior.

J.J.A./R.H.

HEMISPHERE (hem' ə sfir') Hemisphere
means one-half of a sphere or usually one-half of the earth. The earth can be divided into two sections by the equator. The area above the equator is the northern hemisphere, while the area below the equator is the southern hemisphere.

The earth may also be divided into the eastern and western hemispheres. The eastern hemisphere includes Europe, Asia, Africa, and Australia. The western hemisphere includes North and South America. There is no established boundary between the eastern and western hemispheres, although some geographers consider the 20° west longitude and 160° east longitude meridians as the boundary. *See also* LATITUDE AND LONGITUDE; MAP AND MAPPING.

J.M.C./W.R.S.

HEMLOCK (hem' läk) The hemlock is any
of several species of biennial poisonous plants belonging to two genera (plural of genus) of the parsley family. The poison hemlocks belong to genus *Conium*, while the water hemlocks belong to genus *Circuta*.

The most common poison hemlock is *Conium maculatum*. It reaches a height of about 1.2 m [4 ft] and has many branches. The hollow stems usually have red spots. Its leaves are divided and look much like those of the parsley plant. A deadly poison, coniine, is produced by this plant. It is believed that the Greek philosopher Socrates was given a poison hemlock drink as a death sentence.

European water hemlock (*Circuta yirosa*) grows in marshes and is extremely poisonous. American water hemlock (*Circuta maculata*) produces poisonous tubers and leaves. This plant is also called musquash root or beaver poison. *See also* POISONOUS PLANT; PARSLEY FAMILY.   A.J.C./M.H.S.

HEMLOCK TREE The hemolck (hem′ läk) tree is any of 10 species of large, evergreen conifers belonging to the genus *Tsuga* of the pine family. Native to North America, these trees usually have purplish or reddish bark, and long, thin branches. The leaves are short, blunt, and needlelike. Cones grow from the ends of the branches.

The eastern hemlock (*Tsuga canadensis*) reaches heights of about 30 m [100 ft]. Its bark is rich in tannin. (*See* TANNING.) The wood is soft, coarse, and splinters easily. It is often used in building crates. Eastern hemlock is also called Canadian hemlock or hemlock spruce.

The western hemlock (*Tsuga heterophylla*) may be taller than 60 m [200 ft]. Its wood provides valuable lumber. It is also called hemlock fir or Prince Albert's fir.

Although only members of genus *Tsuga* are true hemlocks, some other plants are also called hemlock. *See also* HEMLOCK; PINE FAMILY; YEW.   A.J.C./M.H.S.

HEMOCYANIN (hē′ mō sī′ ə nən) Hemocyanin is a blue pigment found in the blood of some mollusks, the horseshoe crab, and many crustaceans. (*See* PIGMENT.) Like hemoglobin, hemocyanin carries oxygen. It differs from hemoglobin in that it contains copper instead of iron and is dissolved in the blood rather than carried in blood cells. *See also* ARTHROPODA; BLOOD; HEMOGLOBIN; MOLLUSCA.   A.J.C./C.S.H.

HEMOGLOBIN (hē′ mə glō′ bən) Hemoglobin is an iron-containing protein found in the blood of many animals. Its function is to bring oxygen to the tissues of the body. It does this by forming weak, easily broken bonds with oxygen molecules. As the blood travels through the body, these bonds are broken, and hemoglobin gives up the oxygen to the tissues.

In its normal state, hemoglobin is dark blue in color. When it combines with oxygen to form oxyhemoglobin, however, it becomes bright red. It is hemoglobin that gives blood its color. In vertebrates, hemoglobin is part of the red blood cells.

During the formation of the red blood cells in the bone marrow, hemoglobin is also formed. When the red blood cells die, the hemoglobin molecule breaks up. Iron from the hemoglobin goes back to the marrow where it can be used again.

Hemoglobin can also combine with substances other than oxygen. Often, these are permanent bonds which prevent oxygen from combining with the hemoglobin. Because oxygen can no longer get to the tissues, the result may be asphyxiation, or death due to lack of oxygen. Carbon monoxide (found in an automobile's exhaust fumes), for example, replaces oxygen in the hemoglobin molecule, and can cause death. Many poisons also work by replacing the oxygen in a hemoglobin molecule. (*See* ANILINE.)

Several different types of hemoglobin have been identified. Hemoglobin-A is the most common, normal variety. A shortage of hemoglobin-A can result in anemia. Hemoglobin-S is an abnormal type of hemoglobin that is present in sickle cell anemia. This disease is hereditary, and can cause severe pain and death. (*See* HEREDITY.)

A.J.C./J.J.F.

HEMOPHILIA (hē′ mə fil′ ē ə) Hemophilia is a disease of the blood. It is a disorder in which the blood fails to clot, or coagulate, normally. It is due to lack of a substance called antihemophilic factor (AHF) in the bloodstream. AHF is normally made in the liver. It is one of many substances that are necessary for blood to clot properly.

For a person with hemophilia, any cut may prove serious. The wound goes on bleeding, and cannot start to heal. In an ordinary person, a blood clot quickly forms and plugs the wound. The blood dries and goes solid. It prevents further blood loss. If the blood will not clot, even a simple operation like extracting a tooth becomes dangerous. Bleeding into the joints is another danger. A slight knock on the knee, for example, may cause bleeding inside the joint. The joint swells and becomes very painful. Many patients become crippled.

Fortunately it is possible to protect patients to some extent. They can be given transfusions of normal blood before operations, and extra AHF. However, there is no treatment yet that will last for life.

Hemophilia is an inherited disease. It is a disease passed on by the parents. Only males suffer from hemophilia, but females can carry it. A mother may pass it on to her sons without realizing. *See also* GENETICS; HEMORRHAGE; HEREDITY.   D.M.H.W./J.J.F.

HEMORRHAGE (hem′ ə rij) Hemorrhage means bleeding. The word is normally used only when a lot of blood is lost at one time. When an artery is cut, the blood is bright red in color. It spurts out. When a vein is cut, the blood is darker in color, and flows steadily. When the small blood vessels called capillaries are damaged, the blood only oozes out.

A large hemorrhage is very dangerous. A person can bleed to death in less than five minutes if a big artery is damaged. Hemorrhage sometimes occurs inside the body, without being seen. An ulcer can cause bleeding into the stomach or outside it. Hemorrhage from an artery in the brain can cause a stroke. Some diseases make people more likely to have hemorrhages. (*See* HEMOPHILIA.)   D.M.H.W./J.J.F.

HEMP (hemp) Hemp (*Cannabis sativa*) is a tall, annual plant that is usually cultivated for its fibers (also called hemp) or its seeds. It is also the source of the drugs marijuana and hashish. Some botanists classify hemp as a member of the nettle family, others as a member of the mulberry family. Some botanists classify it as a member of a totally separate family (*Cannabaceae*). (*See* CLASSIFICATION OF LIVING ORGANISMS.)

Hemp grows well in subtropical or warm temperate areas. It grows a long tap root. The single stem is hollow and may be as tall as 6 m [20 ft]. The leaves are made up of five or seven leaflets on stalks. The hemp plant is dioecious—that is, either male or female. The male plant has staminate flowers growing in clusters in the axils. The yellowish green flowers have five stamens and five sepals. The female plant has pistillate flowers that are much smaller and less colorful than those of the male plant. The pistillate flowers consist of one sepal wrapped around one pistil.

Hemp fibers are actually long strands of collenchyma growing inside the bark. The fibers are removed by a process called retting. In retting, the stem is soaked or exposed to moisture in the air. This causes the nonfibrous parts to rot. The stem is then beaten to separate the fibers from the rotted matter. Hemp fibers are used in making rope, twine, sailcloth, canvas, and carpets. It is strong, but is not easily bleached or dyed. Although many fibers are incorrectly called hemp, only *Cannabis sativa* produces true hemp fibers.

Hemp seeds are often used as commercial birdfeed. The seeds contain about 30% oil which can be processed into paints or soaps. Frequently, the oil is used for cooking purposes. The hemp plant also produces a resinous oil that is the source of the drug cannabis.

A.J.C./F.W.S.

HENNA (hen′ ə) Henna is an orange red pigment used for coloring hair and fingernails. In some cultures, henna is used to color fingertips, feet, and the manes and hoofs of horses. In the United States, henna is sometimes used to dye wool and silk.

Henna is obtained from the leaves of a small, subtropical shrub, *Lawsonia inermis*, a member of the loosestrife family. This plant has opposite, oval leaves and clusters of fragrant, pink blossoms. It is also called Egyptian privet or Jamaica mignonette. A.J.C./M.H.S.

HENRY (hen′ rē) When an electric current flowing through a loop or coil of wire is changing, an extra induced voltage appears across the loop. (*See* INDUCTION.) The coil is said to have an inductance. This inductance is measured in henries. When the current is changing at one ampere per second and the induced voltage is one volt, the coil has an induction of one henry.

The henry is named after Joseph Henry, an American physicist who pioneered the study of induction in coils. M.E./R.W.L.

HENRY, JOSEPH (1797–1878) Joseph Henry (hen′ rē) was an American physicist. He was born of a poor family in Albany, New York. He was apprenticed to a watchmaker and studied in his spare time. First he studied medicine and then mathematics. Eventually he became a professor at Albany Academy. Henry was interested in magnetism and read about Faraday's discovery of electromagnetic induction in 1831. He discovered self-induction in 1832. Later he designed working electric motors. The unit of inductance is called the henry after him. *See also* INDUCTION. C.M./D.G.F.

HERB (ərb) In botany, herb is usually used in reference to an herbaceous plant. In common usage, however, herbs are plants with scented leaves, roots, or flowers that are used as spices in the preparation of food. Some herbs are used to produce medicines. Although herbs belong to many families, most are members of the mint family and the parsley family. A.J.C./F.W.S.

HERBACEOUS PLANT (ər bā′ shəs plant) Herbaceous plants are plants with soft, green stems. The stems are often juicy or

The giant hogweed is one of the largest of the herbaceous plants, growing to a height of 4.8 m [16 ft]. This biennial plant originated in southwest Asia. Most kinds of herbaceous plants are perennials that survive many winters.

fleshy. Since they contain only small amounts of xylem, the stems are relatively weak. Some herbaceous plants are annuals and die off after one season. Biennial and perennial herbaceous plants, however, lose their stems and branches in the fall and grow new ones in the spring. The roots survive the winter underground. *See also* WOODY PLANT.

A.J.C./M.H.S.

Herbaceous plants, such as the dock (above), lose their stems in fall and grow new ones in spring.

HERBICIDE (ər′ bə sīd′) Herbicides are chemicals which kill plants. Usually, herbicides are used to kill weeds growing among more desirable plants, such as food crops. At one time, sodium chloride (salt) and petroleum based oils were the most widely used herbicides. Since World War II, however, many other substances have been used with much greater control and success.

Herbicides are either selective or non-

selective. Selective herbicides kill certain weeds but do not harm other plants. Non-selective herbicides kill all plants and usually keep other plants from growing. Defoliants and soil sterilants are non-selective herbicides. (*See* CHEMICAL AND BIOLOGICAL WARFARE.)

There are both inorganic and organic herbicides. Inorganic herbicides such as sodium chloride, sulfuric acid, and copper sulfate are usually non-selective. Organic herbicides contain certain chemicals in combination with the elements carbon, hydrogen, and oxygen. Some organic herbicides work by affecting the growth hormones of plants. (*See* GIBBERELLINS.) Others kill selected species of plants by interfering with their metabolism.

Herbicides are chemical weed killers. They are sprayed into the ground before sowing crops. Properly selected, they do not harm crops.

Herbicides are also classified by the way in which they work. Contact herbicides, such as sulfuric acid and paraquat, kill only those parts of a plant with which they come into contact. Contact herbicides are used to kill the above-ground parts of a potato plant before harvesting the underground tubers (potatoes). Translocated herbicides enter through the leaves and are transported throughout the plant, killing the leaves, stems, and roots. (*See* VASCULAR PLANT.) This is especially effective in controlling weeds with extensive roots or rhizomes. Translocated herbicides interfere with the normal biochemistry of the cell, killing the cell and the plant. Residual soil herbicides are usually active over a fairly long period of time. They are added to the soil where they are absorbed by the roots.

Although some herbicides are poisonous to animals and human beings, most are safe if used properly. Herbicides can be sprayed by hand or machine at various times during a plant's life. Modern herbicides have made it possible to keep almost any crop free from weeds from the time it is planted until it is harvested. *See also* FUNGICIDE.

A.J.C./F.W.S.

HERBIVORE (ər′ bə vōr′) An herbivore is any animal that eats only plants. We sometimes call them vegetarians. Well-known herbivores are rabbits, deer, cows, cardinals, squirrels, and honeybees. Herbivores often have specially designed teeth to chew the plants they eat. Their digestive systems have special enzymes to digest the plant matter. *See also* CARNIVORE; INSECTIVORE; OMNIVORE.

S.R.G./M.H.S.

HERCULES (her′ kyə lēz′) Hercules is a constellation visible in the northern sky from April to October. It contains a red giant star that is hundreds of times larger than the sun.

Hercules also contains a globular star cluster called Messier 13. Messier 13 contains about 500,000 stars, yet is barely visible without a telescope. In 1934, a star in Hercules increased in brightness until it appeared brighter than the North Star. It then faded again. Such a star is known as a nova.

Hercules is named for a hero of Greek and Roman mythology.

J.M.C./C.R.

HEREDITY

Heredity (hə red′ ət ē) is the passing of characteristics from parents to offspring. The study of heredity is called genetics. In most cases, the genetic characteristics of an organism are determined when a male gamete (sperm) combines with a female gamete (egg) to form a zygote. (*See* REPRODUCTION.) This zygote has characteristics which it inherits from both parents. As the zygote develops into an embryo, these characteristics become more obvious. These characteristics are controlled by tiny structures called genes. The genes are on chromosomes which are located in every cell of an organism. It is the genes that ''tell'' each cell what it should do in order to become a working part of the organism. (*See* DIFFERENTIATION, CELLULAR.)

The most important work in genetics was that of Gregor Mendel, an Austrian monk. In the 1860s, Mendel developed two laws which helped explain heredity. (*See* MENDEL, GREGOR.)

Mendel's first law Mendel's first law is also called the law of segregation. It states that genes exist in pairs called alleles, one allele on each of a pair of chromosomes. During meiosis, these pairs separate so that only one of these genes is passed from parent to offspring. This gene pairs up with a similar one from the other parent in a process called recombination.

Mendel used pea plants in his experiments because they can either self-fertilize or cross-fertilize. (*See* FERTILIZATION.) He found that if the plants self-fertilized for several generations, the offspring were always identical to the parents. Such offspring were called purebred or homozygous. Mendel then decided to breed two different types of homozygous pea plants—dwarf and tall. The first generation—F_1—produced from this cross were all tall. However, when he allowed members of the F_1 generation to self-fertilize, he found a mixture of tall and dwarf plants in a ratio of 3:1.

These results can be explained by studying the genes of these plants. In peas, there are separate genes which control whether the plant is tall or dwarf. These genes are alleles, located on separate chromosomes of a chromosome pair. A homozygous tall plant has only genes for tallness, and a homozygous dwarf plant has only genes for dwarfness. A hybrid plant is produced by mating a tall plant with a dwarf plant. Genetically, the hybrid is heterozygous. That is, it has one gene for tallness and one gene for dwarfness. The plant appears tall, however, because tallness is dominant over dwarfness. (*See* DOMINANCE.) In the diagrams below, tallness is represented by a red box and dwarfness by a pink circle. All the offspring will be tall in the F₁ generation because they contain the dominant gene for tallness. They also contain the recessive gene for dwarfness.

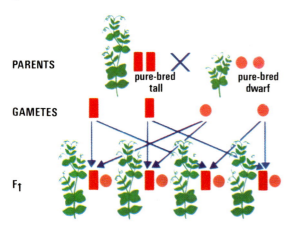

If the F₁ generation is allowed to self-fertilize, the genes on the chromosomes separate into the gametes and recombine again. The second generation of offspring—F₂—will consist of tall and dwarf plants in the ratio 3:1. The tall plants may be either homozygous or heterozygous because tallness is dominant. The dwarf plants, however, are all homozygous because dwarfness is recessive. A recessive characteristic only shows up when an organism is homozygous for that characteristic.

Mendel's second law   Mendel's second law

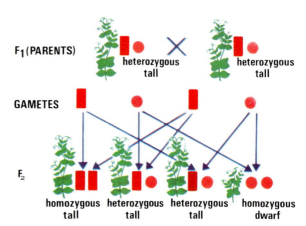

is also called the law of independent assortment. It states that each pair of genes is inherited independently of any other pair of genes. This law is important when studying two or more characteristics at the same time. Mendel used peas with homozygous round, yellow seeds and peas with homozygous wrinkled, green seeds. When he crossed these two, he found that all the offspring (F₁) had round, yellow seeds. This showed that round was dominant over wrinkled, and yellow was dominant over green. When members of the F₁ generation were allowed to self-fertilize, they produced four kinds of seeds: round-yellow, round-green, wrinkled-yellow, and wrinkled-green.

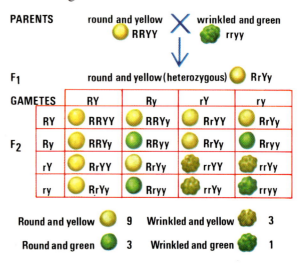

Mendel's second law. The gene for round is dominant over the gene for wrinkled. Yellow is dominant over green. F₂ generation has a 9:3:3:1 ratio.

This law applies only if the two pairs of genes are not linked. Linked genes are located on the same chromosome. They are usually inherited together because it is the chromosomes that separate into the gametes.

Later experiments Although Mendel completed his work in the 1860s, it was ignored until about 1900. In 1910, Thomas Hunt Morgan, an American biologist, was the first to propose the idea of linked genes. (*See* MORGAN, THOMAS HUNT.) He also mapped the locations of genes on the chromosomes. Determining the locus (location) of a gene on a chromosome is called chromosome mapping. Morgan also showed that there can sometimes be an exchange of genes or parts of chromosomes during meiosis. This exchange is called crossing-over.

Other scientists experimented with mutations. Mutations are changes in an offspring caused by changes in the genes. Mutations can cause characteristics in the offspring that were not present in the parents. Mutations occasionally occur naturally, but are more often caused by X rays, drugs, or other factors.

Hereditary diseases Some diseases and disorders are inherited by a child rom his or her parents. Frequently, the disease is caused by recessive genes. In order for the child to have the disease, then, he or she must be homozygous recessive for the disease. Since the normal, non-diseased condition is dominant, heterozygous parents may be carriers, but will have no signs of the disease themselves. Diseases such as hemophilia and sickle cell anemia are hereditary. Some disorders, such as albinism, are also hereditary. (*See* ALBINO.) With some other diseases, such as cancer and diabetes, the tendency to get the disease is inherited, but not the disease itself.

Inheritance The genes which a child receives from his or her parents are the basis for biological inheritance. These are the basic characteristics inherited from the parents. It is the biological inheritance that determines what type of organism develops from a fertilized egg. It also determines the basic physical and mental traits of that organism.

Another major factor in the development of an organism is its environment or cultural inheritance. The environment includes all outside factors from the time the egg is fertilized until the organism dies. Studies have shown that the environment can affect the intelligence, appearance, and other characteristics of an organism. Identical twins have identical biological inheritances. Yet twins who have been raised in separate and different environments have developed into two quite different people. They may have different physical and mental traits which, apparently, are the result of differences in the environment. *See also* BEADLE, GEORGE WELLS; ENZYME.   A.J.C./E.R.L.

HERMAPHRODITE (hər maf′ rə dīt) A hermaphrodite is an organism that has both male and female reproductive organs. (*See* REPRODUCTION.) Many plants are hermaphrodites because their flowers have both stamens (male structures) and pistils (female structures). Monoecious plants have both staminate and pistillate flowers on the same plant. Monoecious plants are also considered to be hermaphrodites.

Many of the lower invertebrates are hermaphrodites. (*See* ANNELIDA; ECHINODERMATA; MOLLUSCA; PLATYHELMINTHES.) Most of these animals are slow moving (for example, snails and slugs) or are attached to some organism or structure (for example, barnacles). Many are parasites. Although hermaphrodites theoretically have the ability to fertilize their own eggs, very few species do. This is often a result of the positions of the reproductive organs. The earthworm, for example, is not able to fertilize itself. Two earthworms, however, can fertilize each

Some hermaphrodites form mating chains, in which each member of the chain fertilizes the next one. Shown is a chain of mating sea hares.

other. Barnacles and other organisms form mating chains, each creature fertilizing the next. Some organisms show successive hermaphroditism. That is, male and female organs develop at different times so that self-fertilization is impossible.

Very few vertebrates are hermaphrodites. Some hermaphroditic fish fertilize their own eggs by laying the eggs and then spreading milt (sperm) over them. As a rule, though, hermaphroditism among vertebrates is rare and is usually abnormal. Occasionally, a human being or a mammal will show pseudohermaphroditism. This means that outwardly, the creature appears to be either male or female. However, the organism has the internal reproductive structures of both sexes. This is extremely rare and is caused by a chromosomal defect. (*See* CHROMOSOME; GENE; HEREDITY.) *See also* FERTILIZATION; MONOECIOUS; POLLINATION; SEX.

A.J.C./E.R.L.

HERMIT CRAB (hər′ mət krab) The hermit crab is a crab in which the hind end of the body is not folded under the rest. Unlike other crabs, the hermit has soft, unprotected rear parts. It protects itself by living inside an empty mollusk shell, such as that of a sea snail. The hermit crab differs from other crabs in having its soft abdomen extended into a snail shell that it carries around. Only the hermit crab's claws remain outside, and form a tightly fitting door. But such a "house" does not grow with the crab. The hermit crab, as it grows, changes its shell for a larger one. Sometimes one hermit crab pulls another one out of the shell it wants. Each hermit crab lives alone in its adopted shell. Large groups of hermit crabs often crowd areas on the bottom of the ocean where seashells are plentiful.

The robber crab, also called the coconut

crab, is a large hermit crab found in the Indo-Pacific region. The robber crab may grow to 61 cm [2 ft] in length. When fully grown, the robber crab gives up living in shells. It developes plates of armor on the rear part of its body. This type of crab lives on land. It is well-known for climbing coconut palms to feed on the nuts.   J.J.A./C.S.H.

The hermit crab protects the soft part of its body by taking over an empty mollusk shell.

HERNIA (hər′ nē ə) A hernia is a bulge in a part of the body. It is caused by an organ pushing through the tissue that normally covers it. Hernias occur most commonly in the abdomen. A loop of intestine may push its way through a weak part of the abdominal wall and form a bulge under the skin. This happens usually in the groin, where the abdomen meets the thigh. Sometimes it happens near the umbilicus. Surgeons can repair hernias by stitching the tissues over the bulge together again. When the bulge is pushed back into place, this is called ''reducing'' the hernia.   D.M.H.W./J.J.F.

HERON (her′ ən) A heron is a bird that belongs to the family Ardeidae. It has a very long neck, a long bill, and long legs. The bird itself may be large or quite small. Herons wade into shallow water and capture small fish for food. They are very graceful and beautiful birds. During the breeding season, many species grow long and colorful feathers or plumes, on their heads. Herons are found all over the world. There are twelve species in North America. The largest is the great white heron. It can grow 95 cm [38 in] tall. It is a pure white bird. Herons spend a great deal of time on the ground, but they fly well. They fly with their necks bent in an S-shaped curve with their heads drawn back. Bitterns and egrets are types of herons. *See also* CRANE; EGRET.   S.R.G./L.L.S.

Herons are long-legged wading birds that live in most warm parts of the world. Two of the many species are the lined tiger heron, shown at the left, and the agami heron, shown below.

HERPETOLOGY (hər pə täl′ ə jē) The study of amphibians and reptiles is called herpetology. A scientist who studies amphibians and reptiles is called a herpetologist. Herpetologists study many different things about the animals. They study how their bodies are put together, how they are related to other animals, and how and where they live. By learning more about amphibians and reptiles, scientists also learn more about the earth around us and its past. *See also* AMPHIBIAN; ANATOMY; EVOLUTION; REPTILE.

A.R.G./R.L.L.

HERRING (her' ing) The herring is a saltwater fish that belongs to the family Clupeidae. is a silvery fish that grows to about 30 cm [12 in] in length. Herrings are found in the northern waters of both the Atlantic and Pacific Oceans. They swim in huge schools—groups of thousands of fish. Herring feed on plankton, small animals floating in the water. (*See* PLANKTON.) The herring is a valuable food fish. *See also* SHAD.   S.R.G./E.C.M.

HERSCHEL, SIR JOHN FREDERICK WILLIAM (1792–1871) Sir John Herschel (hər' shəl) was a British astronomer. He build an observatory at Feldhausen near the Cape of Good Hope, South Africa. From there he made the first telescopic survey of the southern sky. He was also a chemist and invented ways of photographing stars. His father was Sir William Herschel. C.M./D.G.F.

John Herschel

HERTZ (herts) The frequency of a wave is the number of vibrations, or cycles, passing a stationary observer in one second. Frequency is measured in hertz, abbreviated Hz. The old name for this unit is cycles per second. This unit is named after the German physicist, Heinrich Hertz, who was the first to produce electromagnetic waves. (*See* HERTZ, HEINRICH.)   M.E./R.W.L.

HERTZ, HEINRICH (1857–1894) Heinrich Hertz (herts) was a German physicist. He was born in Hamburg. Hertz was the first person to prove the existence of electromagnetic radiation. He found that he could detect a spark jumping between two charged rods. He used a copper ring with a small gap in it. When the spark jumped between the rods, a spark also passed over the gap in the copper ring. The ring was several meters away from the rods. Hertz deduced that some kind of radiation went through the air. This was the discovery from which radio was invented. *See also* ELECTROMAGNETIC RADIATION; RADIO.

C.M./D.G.F.

Heinrich Hertz, a German physicist of the later 1800s, laid the foundation for Marconi's invention of the radio by showing that electromagnetic radiation exists.

HIBERNATION (hī' bər nā' shən) Hibernation is a deep sleep that some animals go into during the winter. In the winter, many animals have trouble finding food. Since the weather is cold, their bodies use much more energy than usual just to keep warm. For many animals, hibernation is the only way to survive during this time.

Before an animal hibernates, it eats a great deal of food. Much of this food is stored as fat

All amphibians and reptiles in the colder parts of the world hibernate during the winter. Frogs usually do this by burying themselves at the bottom of a pond, on the surface of the mud, or under damp grass.

in the animal's body. This fat is used as a source of energy during hibernation. During hibernation, an animal's rate of metabolism is greatly reduced. (*See* METABOLISM.) The body temperature is much lower than normal, and is usually about the same as the air temperature. The rates of respiration and breathing slow down. (*See* RESPIRATION.) The heart also slows down. (*See* CIRCULATORY SYSTEM.) The animal's control systems, however, remain active. For example, if the weather becomes too cold, the rate of metabolism increases, body temperature rises, more stored fat is used, and circulation and respiration increase. As a result, the animal wakes up and can move to a warmer place, if necessary.

Scientists are not sure of the exact cause of hibernation. Hibernation may be brought on by environmental changes—lower temperatures, shorter days, and less food available. These environmental changes may trigger changes in the functioning of the animal's hypothalamus (part of the brain) or adrenal glands. The end of hibernation may also be environmentally directed, but the true hibernators seem to be able to wake up whenever they want to.

The only true hibernators are several warm-blooded animals. These include some birds (such as the swift) and some mammals (such as the bat, hamster, lemur, marmot, and ground squirrel). The body temperature of a warm-blooded animal usually stays fairly constant and is not greatly affected by the air temperature. During true hibernation, the animal's body temperature drops to well below normal. Most true hibernators actually go through a series of shorter naps rather than one long, uninterrupted sleep.

Many cold-blooded animals enter a type of hibernation. Since the body temperature of these animals is usually close to the air temperature anyway, it is not considered to be a true hibernation. All amphibians and reptiles living in cold areas sleep through the winter. Some bury themselves in the soil or at the bottom of a pond to keep from being frozen. When the weather warms up, the metabolic rate increases gradually and the animal becomes active again. Many insects spend the winter in one of the earlier stages of metamorphosis (egg, larva, or pupa). (*See* METAMORPHOSIS.)

Some animals, such as bears, sleep during the winter, but their body temperature stays near normal. This type of winter sleep is called carnivorean lethargy. Some animals enter a true hibernation every day. Bats, for example, hibernate during the day and become active at night. This is known as diurnal hibernation.

Other animals enter a deep sleep during the summer, particularly when the weather is very hot and water is scarce. This summer sleep is called estivation. Many desert animals estivate. Also, animals that live in or near the water may estivate if their water source dries up. *See also* DORMANCY.

A.J.C./R.J.B.

HIBISCUS (hī bis′ kəs) Hibiscus is a genus of 200 to 300 species of flowering plants belonging to the mallow family. Some are herbaceous plants, while others are trees or shrubs. (*See* WOODY PLANT.) They grow in tropical and temperate regions throughout the world. The leaves are usually toothed and divided. The large, bell-shaped flowers are

Plants and shrubs of the genus *hibiscus* have large, five-petaled flowers.

made up of five petals which may be white, yellow, pink, or red.

The swamp rose mallow (*Hibiscus moscheutos*) is common in marshes in the eastern United States. Its white or pink flowers often measure more than 18 cm [7 in] across. *Hibiscus esculentus* produces a seed pod called okra or gumbo. It is a popular food in many parts of the country, and is often cooked in stews or soups. *See also* MALLOW FAMILY.

A.J.C./M.H.S.

HICKORY (hik′ rē) The hickory is a tree that grows throughout the eastern United States. It has long leaves made up of many smaller leaflets. The hickories also produce large nuts which are eaten by wildlife and people. There are ten species of hickories in North America. The pecan tree is a type of hickory. The wood of hickory trees is used for the handles of tools such as axes and hammers because it is very strong. S.R.G./M.H.S.

HI-FI (hī′ fī′) Hi-fi, or high fidelity, is a way of reproducing sound with the greatest possible fidelity (faithfulness) to the original. Hi-fi equipment can be used to reproduce any kind of sound, but is most often used for music. The best hi-fi equipment can make recorded or broadcast music sound almost the way it sounds in a concert hall.

A sound reproduction system must meet three basic requirements to qualify as a high fidelity system. (1) It must be able to reproduce every musical tone that is heard in the concert hall. (2) It must reproduce loud tones as clearly as soft ones. (3) It should not produce any noise or other sounds of its own while playing.

Today, most hi-fi sets are built to reproduce stereophonic sound, or stereo. A stereo system adds realism by reproducing sounds from their proper directions. If the brass section is on the right side of the concert hall, the sound of the brass section comes out of the right speaker, or right side of the stereo set.

The basic parts of a hi-fi system are the program source, amplifier, and loudspeaker system. The program source can be a record player, an FM (frequency modulated) radio tuner, or tape recording equipment.

In a record player, the pickup cartridge in the player's tone arm produces weak electrical waves when the record makes the needle vibrate from side to side, or up and down. (*See* RECORD PLAYER.) An FM tuner changes a radio broadcast into similar electric waves. Tape recording equipment changes magnetic patterns on a tape into electric waves. (*See* TAPE RECORDER.) To re-create sound from any of these sources, the electric waves are connected to the amplifier, which, in turn, is connected to the loudspeaker system.

The first part of the amplifier that the waves enter is the preamplifier. The preamplifier strengthens the waves. It also has controls with which to adjust the volume and the tone of the sound. The other part of the amplifier, the power amplifier, makes the electric waves powerful enough to drive, or operate, the loudspeaker. The loudspeaker changes the electrical waves into sound. In some hi-fi systems the preamplifier and power amplifier are separate parts.

Most hi-fi systems are sold complete and ready to play. However, some people build their own components and put together a system. Transistors have helped manufacturers combine hi-fi components in the same cabinet. Transistors are small devices that eliminate large, heavy parts used in components once made with vacuum tubes.

Stereophonic hi-fi gives relative depth and clarity to sounds by reproducing them from their proper directions. Engineers use at least two microphones when recording an orchestra in stereo. They place one microphone on the left side of the orchestra, and one on the right side. The sound waves picked up by the left microphone make up the left stereo channel, and those picked up by the right microphone make up the right channel. The sounds come out of the stereo speakers that way. Four-channel stereo, also called quadraphonic stereo, involves the use of four microphones in the recording phase, and four loudspeakers for playback. Two-channel stereo can be broadcast on FM stereo radio. Four-channel stereo is available only on records and tapes.

A hi-fi system needs a stereo amplifier to reproduce both channels. A stereo amplifier actually contains two amplifiers, one for the right channel and one for the left channel. Each amplifier is attached to its own loudspeaker. The speakers are usually placed several feet apart in a room to enhance the stereo effect. Four-channel amplifiers contain four amplifiers within the same cabinet. Each amplifier has its own loudspeaker. The loudspeakers are usually placed in the four corners of a room.

Components of a modern hi-fi system.

Manufacturers began producing the first hi-fi equipment around 1948, when long playing (LP) records first became available. Hi-fi equipment had been used only in radio stations and recording studios up to that time. It was too expensive for home use. FM radio began in the early 1940s, and FM stations began to experiment with stereo broadcasting in the early 1950s. They broadcast one channel of sound over FM, and the other over AM (amplitude modulation) radio or the audio part of television. Stereophonic records were introduced in 1958 and created a tremendous demand for stereo hi-fi home systems.

The first multiplex stereo broadcasts took place in 1961. In this system, one FM station broadcasts both channels. Four-channel stereo was introduced in 1969. *See also* LOUDSPEAKER; RADIO; SOUND.

W.R.P./L.L.R.

HIPPARCHUS (about 160–about 126 BC)

Hipparchus (hi pär′ kəs) was a Greek astronomer. All that we know about him comes from the writings of Ptolemy. Ptolemy tells us that Hipparchus built an observatory at Rhodes. He is the earliest systematic astronomer we know about. He discovered the precession of the equinoxes and catalogued more than a thousand stars. Hipparchus must have been a brilliant mathematician as well as an outstanding scientist. He invented trigonometry and worked out the distances of the sun and moon from earth. He also used a system of latitude and longitude to show where places on earth are. *See also* EQUINOX; PTOLEMY; TRIGONOMETRY.   C.M./D.G.F.

HIPPOCRATES (about 470–about 377 BC)

Hippocrates (hi pŏk′ rə tēz) was a Greek doctor. He was born on the island of Cos. He is called "the father of medicine." Modern medical students make a promise to be ethical in their work. This is called the Hippocratic Oath.

Hippocrates is supposed to have written a large number of books. Most of these were probably written by other doctors working on Cos at the same time. They are known as the Hippocratic School. Some of the descriptions of diseases in these books are very clear and accurate. The diseases can be recognized today. No other medical books as scientific as these were written until modern times.

C.M./D.G.F.

HIPPOPOTAMUS (hip′ ə pät′ ə məs) Hip-

popotamus is the name given to two species of huge land mammals native to central and western Africa. Although its name comes from two Greek words meaning "water horse," the hippopotamus is more closely related to the pig than to the horse. The river hippopotamus (*Hippopotamus amphibius*) is also called the great African hippopotamus. It has a large body, short legs, and feet with webbed toes. It may grow to be 5 m [16.5 ft] long and 1.5 m [5 ft] tall at the shoulder. The largest weigh close to 3,000 kg [6,600 lb]. The eyes, ears, and nostrils all stick out from the top of the head. This allows the animal to see, hear, and breathe while most of its body is under water. The hippopotamus has special oil glands to keep the grayish skin moist. The oil is sometimes red, giving rise to the incorrect belief that the animal sweats blood.

The hippopotamus has large, curved teeth. Its canine teeth are enlarged into tusks which may be 60 cm [2 ft] long. The hippopotamus is a good swimmer and, on land, can run as fast as 48 km [30 mi] per hour. Hippopotamuses roam in herds of as many as 30 animals, spending most of the day in the water. At night, hippopotamuses leave the water and graze on land, often causing great destruction to cultivated crops. An average hippopotamus eats about 60 kg [132 lb] of food each day.

A female hippopotamus first mates when she is five or six years old. After a gestation period of about eight months, she gives birth to one calf. The newborn calf may weigh as much as 50 kg [110 lb]. The calf is able to swim almost immediately. It nurses underwater, surfacing every few minutes for air. Hippopotamuses live for about 30 years.

The pygmy hippopotamus (*Cheoropsis liberiensis*) is much smaller and darker than the river hippopotamus. It weighs about 230 kg [506 lb] and is about 1.8 m [6 ft] long. It stands only 75 cm [2.5 ft] tall at the shoulder. This animal spends relatively little time in the water, and usually wanders through forests and grasslands.

Hippopotamuses are widely hunted for their hides, meat, and ivory tusks. Although protected by law in most places, these animals are often killed illegally. The pygmy hippopotamus is an endangered species and may soon be extinct.   A.J.C./J.J.M.

The hippopotamus is related to the pig. Hippos spend most of their time in water.

HISTOLOGY (his täl′ ə jē) Histology is the study of plant and animal tissue. Tissue is a group of cells that work together to perform a specific function. Histologists examine tissue to learn about its structure, functions, and its properties. Valuable information about diseases has been obtained through histological research. The chief tool of the histologist is the microscope.   J.M.C./E.R.L.

HOFMANN, AUGUST (1818–1892) August Hofmann (hōf′ män) was a German chemist. He made many important discoveries in organic chemistry. He is famous for the Hofmann degradation reaction. This is a way of changing an organic compound by removing a carbon atom from each molecule. Hofmann developed aniline dyes from coal products. These are called Hofmann violets. He also discovered formaldehyde and styrene.   C.M./D.G.F.

HOLLY FAMILY The holly (häl′ ē) family includes 295 species of evergreen trees and shrubs with shiny green leaves and red fruits. The name probably comes from the fact that these popular Christmas plants were once thought to be holy trees. They have alternate, simple leaves, and flowers clustered in the axils. Most members of the holly family are dioecious. That is, each plant has either male flowers or female flowers, but not both.

The American holly (*Ilex opaca*) may grow to a height of 30 m [100 ft]. Its red fruits are called berries, but they are actually drupes. The fruits are poisonous and grow only on the female trees (with the pistillate flowers). English holly (*Ilex aquifolium*) is a popular shrub that is often grown with hawthorn in hedges. The wood from members of the holly family is very hard. It is used in making musical instruments and furniture.   A.J.C./M.H.S.

European holly, species *Ilex aquifolium*.

HOLLYHOCK (häl′ ē häk′) Hollyhock (*Althaea rosea*) is a herbaceous plant belonging to the mallow family. Though native to China, it is widely cultivated in the United States for its spikes of colorful red, pink, purple, or yellow flowers. The large (7.5 cm

[3 in]) blossoms grow from the axils near the top of a thick stem. This stem with its spike of flowers may grow to be as tall as 2.7 m [9 ft]. The leaves are usually large, hairy, and heart-shaped with five to seven lobes. Though most varieties are perennial, some are annual or biennial. *See also* INFLORESCENCE; MALLOW FAMILY. A.J.C./M.H.S.

HOLMIUM (hōl′ mē əm) Holmium (Ho) is a bright silvery metallic element. The atomic number of holmium is 67 and its atomic weight is 164.93. It melts at 1,474°C [2,685°F] and boils at 2,695°C [4,883°F]. Its relative density is 8.8. It is one of the rare earth group of metals and is obtained from the mineral monazite. Holmium was discovered by the Swiss chemist J. L. Soret in 1878. No important uses have yet been discovered for the metal. M.E./J.R.W.

HOLOGRAPHY (hō läg′ rə fē) Holography is a method of recording and viewing a three-dimensional image. The image is recorded onto a photographic plate called a hologram. The hologram is then used to reproduce the image. The image is not like an ordinary photograph, or the image on a television screen. The image is three-dimensional. This means that the image changes when you look at it from different angles. If the image is of an object, then the object appears to be solid.

Holography was invented in 1947 by a British electrical engineer, Denis Gabor. In holography, a beam of electromagnetic radiation is used. This beam must be of one wavelength. (*See* FREQUENCY.) White light, for example, could not be used, since it is a mixture of light of different wavelengths. Pure red light could be used, since it only has one wavelength. The radiation must also be coherent. This means that the crests and troughs of all the waves must coincide. Ordinary light cannot be used because it is not coherent. In 1960, the laser was invented. (*See* LASER.) Lasers produce coherent light and so can be used to produce visible, three-dimensional images.

Holograms are very useful to scientists. They can quickly record an object or a scene and it will all be in focus. In an ordinary photograph, part of the picture is usually out of focus. Certain types of holograms can be used to store information for computers. Other uses for holography could be developed in the future. For example, holograms could be used to produce three-dimensional television or motion pictures.

This diagram shows how a hologram, a three-dimensional image, is recorded and reproduced.

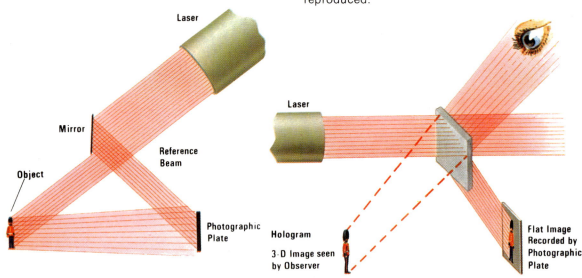

Laser

Mirror

Object

Reference Beam

Photographic Plate

Laser

Hologram

3-D Image seen by Observer

Flat Image Recorded by Photographic Plate

How holography works Holography works by using an effect in physics called interference. (*See* INTERFERENCE.) In interference, two coherent waves with the same wavelength combine together. They can combine in different ways. The crests and troughs of each wave can coincide. In this case, the combined wave is as bright as the two waves when they are separate. Or the crests of one wave can combine with the troughs of the other. In this case, the two waves cancel each other out and there is no combined wave. In this way, the two waves combine to produce a pattern of light and dark patches. This is called an interference pattern.

In holography, a beam of light from a laser is split by a mirror. Part of the beam lights up the scene to be recorded. This part of the beam then hits a photographic plate. The other part of the beam is reflected by the mirror straight onto the plate. This beam is called the reference beam. The two beams interfere with each other and the interference pattern is recorded on the photographic plate. The plate can now be used as a hologram.

To view the scene, light from a laser is shone onto the hologram. The hologram behaves like a diffraction grating. (*See* DIFFRACTION.) The hologram causes the beam to be split up into different beams. One of these beams produces a flat image which can be photographed. Another beam produces a three-dimensional image, which seems to lie directly behind the hologram.　M.E./S.S.B.

HOMEOSTASIS (hō′ mē ō stā′ səs) Homeostasis is the ability of a living thing to keep a steady, stable condition within its body. This internal environment is controlled by different body processes, such as respiration, circulation, and balance of body fluids. The nervous system and the hormones of the endocrine system play a major part in homeostasis. The excretion of wastes is an important part of homeostasis. In warm-blooded animals, excretion helps to maintain a constant body temperature.

Scientists believe that homeostasis shows the degree of evolution of a species. The steadier a living thing's internal systems are, the more independent it is of the external environment, and the more developed (advanced) it is.

The maintenance of social structures in populations of organisms is also regarded as homeostasis between organisms. *See also* ENVIRONMENT.　J.J.A./E.R.L.

HOMOLOGUE (hō′ mə lòg′) In organic chemistry, certain compounds can be grouped together. These groups are called homologous series. A compound that belongs to such a group is called a homologue, or homolog. An example of a homologous series is the alkanes or paraffins. The first member is

Each chemical compound in a group is a homologue of others in the series.

methane. Its chemical formula is CH_4. Next comes ethane (C_2H_6), then propane (C_3H_8), and so on. In this example, the formula for each homologue differs from the next by CH_2. This is true for all homologous series. Other homologous series include the alcohols, the aldehydes, and the alkenes, or olefins. Homologues have similar chemical properties and their physical properties change as you move through the series. For example, the melting and boiling points become higher. In the paraffins, the lowest members are gases. As you move through the series, they become liquids at normal temperatures, and then solids. M.E./J.M.

HONEY LOCUST (hən′ ē lō′ kəst) The honey locust is a tree that grows in the central United States. It grows to about 24 m [80 ft] tall. The leaves of the honey locust resemble a fern. Many—but not all—honey locust trees have thorns on their branches. The seeds of the tree are grown inside a dark brown pod that looks like a large string bean. The honey locust is common around lakes and streams. *See also* FERN. S.R.G./M.H.S.

HONEYSUCKLE FAMILY The honeysuckle (hən′ ē sək′ əl) family includes about 350 species of flowering dicotyledons. Most are shrubs or climbing plants native to temperate areas throughout the world. Two common shrubs in this family are the viburnum and the elder. (*See* ELDERBERRY.)

The honeysuckles belong to the genus *Lonicera*. Most are evergreens with opposite, dark green, oval leaves. The flowers are trumpet-shaped with four petals above and one petal below. The petals form a long tube which makes it difficult for most insects to pollinate them. Hawk moths and hummingbirds are the usual agents of pollination because they are able to reach into the base of the flower to get the nectar. The flowers give rise to red, orange, or black berries.

(*See* FRUIT.) These berries are a popular food of birds.

The common honeysuckle (*Lonicera periclymenum*) is a climbing plant that grows to a height of about 6 m [20 ft]. It has clusters of yellowish flowers with purple edges. The sweet honeysuckle (*Lonicera caprifolium*) has clustered, purplish white flowers which open at night and close during the day. *See also* ADAPTATION. A.J.C./M.H.S.

The common honeysuckle, *Lonicera periclymenum*.

HOOKE, ROBERT (1635–1703) Robert Hooke (hùk) was an English scientist. He made discoveries in many branches of physics and chemistry. He was also a clever designer. He helped Robert Boyle to design an air pump. His work was also useful in the designing of Newcomen's steam engine. In 1660, Hooke discovered that the strain on a material is proportional to the stress. This is called Hook's law. (*See* ELASTICITY.) The strain is the ratio of the amount it stretches to the original length. The stress is the force per unit area applied. He made the first Gregorian telescope and also designed buildings.

C.M./D.G.F.

The microscope used by Robert Hooke in his studies of plant cells.

HOP (häp) Hop is one of four species of herbaceous plants belonging to the genus *Humulus*. Closely related to hemp, it also is classified in one of three families: mulberry family, nettle family, or the family Cannabaceae. (*See* CLASSIFICATION OF LIVING ORGANISMS.) Hops are native to temperate areas throughout the world.

The common hop (*Humulus lupulus*) is a tall, perennial, climbing plant with large, toothed leaves. It is a dioecious plant with either staminate (male) flowers in clusters or pistillate (female) flowers in a cone-shaped catkin. This catkin is covered with thin scales called bracts. The catkins are dried and used in brewing beer. *See also* HEMP. A.J.C./F.W.S.

HORIZON (hə rīz′ ən) The horizon is where the land or sea seems to meet the earth. It is also called the visible horizon. At sea, where there are no visual obstructions, the horizon appears about 4 km [2.5 mi] away.

The horizon appears farther away when viewed from a high place. This is because the earth is round. For example, an airplane pilot flying at a height of 1.6 km [1 mi] sees the horizon 158 km [98 mi] away. This is because the pilot is seeing farther over the curvature of the earth than a viewer at sea level.

The celestial horizon is the circle at which a plane, passing through the observer's location at a right angle to a point directly overhead, meets the celestial sphere. The celestial horizon is also called the astronomical horizon. *See also* CELESTIAL SPHERE; ZENITH.

J.M.C./C.R.

HORMONE

A hormone (hôr′ mōn′) is a chemical substance that is produced in one part of an organism and has an effect on another part of that organism. Both plants and animals produce hormones. Hormones are vital body substances that act as ''chemical messengers'' to control body development and function. (*See* HOMEOSTASIS.)

Plant hormones Hormones are important in the growth and development of plants. Most plant hormones are concentrated in the growing regions such as the tips of stems and roots. The major plant hormones are auxins, cytokinins, and gibberellins. Auxins have several functions including causing the elongation of cells and the development of fruit. Auxins produced in the tip of the stem (the coleoptile) prevent side or lateral branches from growing. This is known as apical dominance. Auxins are also responsible for the tropisms. (*See* MOVEMENT OF PLANTS.) Cytokinins work closely with auxins by controlling cellular division and cellular differentiation. (*See* MITOSIS.) Gibberellins cause a plant to grow larger. All three of these hormones are closely related. Growth of a plant is controlled by the balance of these hormones.

Human hormones   Most human hormones are produced by the endocrine or ductless glands. They are called ductless because they secrete hormones directly into the blood, and not into tubes or other structures. The blood carries the hormones throughout the body until they reach the "target" organ or tissue. Although the amount of each hormone in the blood is very tiny, it is tightly controlled within certain limits. Too much or too little of a hormone often has a harmful effect on the body. The major endocrine glands are the pituitary, the thyroid, four parathyroid glands, two adrenal glands, the islets of Langerhans, and the thymus gland.

The pituitary gland is located at the base of the brain. It is sometimes called the master gland because it secretes hormones which control most of the other glands. The pituitary itself is controlled by the hypothalamus, part of the brain. The pituitary has three sections: the anterior lobe, the intermediate lobe, and the posterior lobe. The anterior lobe produces six hormones. Adrenocorticotropic hormone (ACTH) controls the cortex of the adrenal glands. Thyroid stimulating hormone (TSH) controls the thyroid gland. Follicle stimulating hormone (FSH) and luteinizing hormone (LH) control the sex glands. Prolactin stimulates the production of milk in a mother who is breast-feeding her child. Growth hormone (GH) is sometimes called somatotropin. GH controls growth by controlling the way the body uses food in building tissues. Too much GH can cause a person to become a giant. Too little can cause a person to be a dwarf. If a large, abnormal amount of GH is produced in an adult, the result can be acromegaly.

The only hormone produced by the intermediate lobe is melanocyte stimulating hormone (MSH). In some vertebrates MSH controls pigment in the skin. The function of MSH in human beings, however, is unknown.

The posterior lobe produces two hormones. Vasopressin is also called antidiuretic hormone (ADH). ADH controls the amount of water present in the blood. Too little ADH can result in the disease diabetes insipidus. This disease is characterized by the loss of great amounts of water. It can lead to dehydration and death. Oxytocin causes the muscles of the uterus to contract when a pregnant woman begins labor. (*See* PREGNANCY.) It also helps cause the release of milk as a mother breast-feeds her baby. Recent experiments indicate that these two hormones are actually produced by the hypothalamus, and are simply stored in the posterior lobe of the pituitary.

The thyroid gland is located on both sides of the trachea in the throat. It produces two hormones which control body metabolism. Thyroxine and triiodothyronine regulate the rate at which cells use food to produce energy. Too much of these hormones can cause the condition known as exophthalmia, or bulging eyes. Over-production causes increased metabolism which results in nervousness, weight loss, weakness, and increased heartbeat. Too little of these hormones may cause the disease myxedema. This is characterized by decreased metabolism and results in sluggishness, weight gain, slow heartbeat, and general tiredness. In order for the thyroid gland to function properly, there must be enough iodine in the diet. Iodine is commonly added to table salt to prevent this deficiency. (*See* SODIUM CHLORIDE.) If there is a lack of iodine, goiter, or swelling of the thyroid gland, may result. If a pregnant woman has too little iodine in her diet, her child may be affected by cretinism. Cretinism results in mental and physical retardation.

The parathyroid glands are embedded in the thyroid gland. They produce parathyroid hormone or parathormone. This hormone controls the usage of calcium and phosphorous in the body. These minerals are vital for proper functioning of muscles, bones, and nerves. Too little parathormone can result in tetany, a general contracting of muscles which eventually can cause death. Too much parathormone can cause an excess of calcium in the blood. This results in kidney and bladder stones, kidney failure, increased blood pressure, and blood clots.

The adrenal glands are located on top of the kidneys. These glands have two sections: the outer adrenal cortex and the inner adrenal medulla. The adrenal cortex produces several hormones. Corticosterone and cortisol control the metabolism of carbohydrates, fats, and proteins. Aldosterone controls the salt balance in the body. (*See* SODIUM; POTASSIUM.) Androgen, like androsterone, is a male sex hormone. An injury or disease which affects the adrenal cortex may result in the underproduction of these hormones. This condition is called Addison's disease.

The adrenal medulla produces two hormones. Epinephrine and norepinephrine are also called adrenalin and noradrenalin. These hormones stimulate the nervous system in times of great stress. They increase the heart rate and the amount of energy available to the muscles.

The sex glands are the testes (testicles) and the ovaries. The testes produce testosterone, a male sex hormone. The ovaries produce three hormones. Estriol (an estrogen) and progesterone control the menstrual cycle. Progesterone is also important during pregnancy. Relaxin helps widen the birth canal (vagina) just before the birth of a baby.

The islets of Langerhans are part of the pancreas. They produce two hormones. Insulin decreases the amount of sugar in the blood. Too little insulin results in the disease diabetes mellitus. (*See* DIABETES.) Too much insulin can cause the disease hypoglycemia which is characterized by low blood sugar. Glucagon balances insulin, performing the opposite function. Glucagon releases sugar into the blood.

The thymus gland is located in the chest. It is large in infants and gets smaller as the child grows older. The thymus produces thymosin. Although its function is not clearly understood, thymosin apparently helps protect babies from disease. (*See* IMMUNITY.)

There are other hormones which are not produced by the endocrine glands. The hormones produced by the stomach, duodenum, and small intestines function in the digestion of food. They control the production of digestive juices.

Hormones in other animals Most mammals produce hormones similar to those of human beings. Other vertebrates and some invertebrates also produce hormones, though not as much is known about their functions. Pheromones are special hormones released into the environment by fish, insects, and other animals. Pheromones signal others of the same species and may be a mating signal or a warning of danger. The process of metamorphosis is also controlled by hormones.

How hormones work Hormones are generally divided into two groups. The steroids, such as produced by the sex glands and the adrenal cortex, are relatively simple chemicals. The rest of the hormones are polypeptides, and are similar to amino acids and proteins.

Hormones work by changing the chemical activities in a cell. It is thought that the steroids enter the cell and affect the genes directly. Polypeptide hormones, however, stay outside the cell and attach to the cell membrane. This affects the enzymes, causing the production of a substance called cyclic AMP inside the cell. Cyclic AMP then causes chemical changes in the cell.

Uses of hormones Realizing the importance of hormones, scientists have tried to develop synthetic substitutes for the hormones. These can be used to treat hormonal deficiencies which may have been caused by malfunction, injury, or disease of one of the endocrine glands. In addition, hormones have been shown effective in treating other diseases. For example, cortisone is often used as a treatment for arthritis and allergies. Synthetic sex hormones are used in birth control pills. Birth control pills prevent a woman from producing an egg, and thus prevent her from becoming pregnant. (*See* CONTRACEPTION.) Synthetic plant hormones have been used for many years to increase crop production. Other hormones are fed to livestock to make them grow more quickly and produce more meat. A.J.C./J.J.F.

HORNBEAM (hòrn' bēm') The hornbeam is a small tree that grows in the central and eastern United States. It rarely exceeds 12 m [40 ft] in height. There are two species of hornbeam: the American hornbeam and the eastern hop hornbeam. Both have very tough wood which is often used for handles of tools. The seeds are eaten by many songbirds and other wildlife. The trunk of the American hornbeam is very smooth with wide ridges. S.R.G./M.H.S.

HORNBILL (hòrn' bil') The hornbills are 45 species of tropical African and Asian birds that belong to the family Bucerotidae. They have huge bills which are usually filled with air spaces and covered with a thin layer of hard, bonelike material. These air spaces keep the bill lightweight. Hornbills have large heads and wings and long tails. They range in size from 38 to 150 cm [15 to 60 in] in length. Their feathers are usually brown or black with white markings. Most hornbills live in the tops of trees and eat fruits and insects.

In most species, a female lays her eggs in a hollow tree. The male then fills up the opening in the tree with clay and mud, locking the female and her eggs inside. A small hole is left so that the male can feed the female while she stays with the eggs. After the eggs have hatched, the male helps the female break out of her ''prison.'' They may then fill in the opening again, leaving the baby hornbills inside. The adults feed the babies through a small hole until the babies are almost fully grown. The young hornbills are then freed. *See also* BIRD; TOUCAN. A.J.C./L.L.S.

HORNBLENDE (hòrn' blend') Hornblende is a shiny green, brown, or black mineral. It often occurs in the form of dark, needlelike crystals. Hornblende is a common mineral in igneous and metamorphic rocks. Some metamorphic rocks are composed entirely of hornblende. The chemical composition of hornblende is quite variable. It is a silicate and contains aluminum and other elements, such as sodium, potassium, iron, and magnesium. *See also* SILICA. J.J.A./R.H.

HORNET (hòr' nət) Hornet is the name given to several species of large wasps. They are social insects that live in papery nests made from plant fibers which have been chewed and formed into a papier-mâché-like substance. A hornet colony consists of one or more queens (fertile females), many workers (sterile females), and, at times, several males. A queen starts the colony by building a small nest in which she lays only a few eggs. The unfertilized eggs develop into larvae which mature into workers. (*See* PARTHENOGENESIS.) The workers then increase the size of the nest, feed the queen and any developing larvae, and protect the nest. The queen now only lays eggs. By the end of the summer, a single nest may have thousands of worker hornets.

With colder weather, the queen leaves the nest to hibernate in a protected place. (*See* HIBERNATION.) All of the other hornets die, and the nest is abandoned. Next spring, the process is repeated as the queen comes out of hibernation and starts another nest. Hornets rarely use the same nest twice.

Two common hornets are the white-faced hornet (*Vespula maculata*) and the giant hornet (*Vespa crabro*). The giant hornet is also called the yellow jacket. Hornets are aggressive and dangerous insects. They sting by inserting the stinger and then injecting a poison. This poison causes swelling and intense pain. Hornet larvae, however, are helpful creatures as they feed on flies, caterpillars, and other harmful insects. *See also* WASP.

A.J.C./J.E.R.

HORSE (hôrs) The horse (*Equus caballus*) is an ungulate, or hoofed mammal, belonging to the order Perissodactyla. It evolved from a small animal called eohippus that lived in North America and Europe more than 50 million years ago. (*See* EVOLUTION.)

Horses range in size from the largest, the draft horses, at 1,100 kg [2,420 lb] to the smallest, the Shetland ponies, at 140 kg [308 lb]. The height of a horse is measured in hands from the ground to the withers, a point between the shoulder blades on the back of the horse. A hand is the average width of a man's hand, or 10 cm [4 in]. The largest draft horses grow to a height of 20 hands (200 cm [6 ft 8 in]). The average horse is about 15.2 hands (155 cm [5 ft 2 in]) tall. Any full-grown horse that is shorter than 14.2 hands (147 cm [4 ft 10 in]) tall is called a pony.

A horse's body is covered with hair that may be a solid or mixed color, or may be spotted or splotched. It has a long tail which is used to brush away insects. The horse has large, keen eyes which can move in opposite directions at the same time. Its ears can be moved to "catch" faint sounds. Most male horses (stallions) have 40 teeth, while most females (mares) have 36 teeth. The age and health of a horse can be determined by counting the number of teeth and examining their condition.

The legs of a horse are well-suited for running. (*See* ADAPTATION.) The front legs are thinner than the hind legs and can withstand the shock of absorbing the horse's weight. The hind legs are larger and more muscular to provide the strength needed for running and jumping. The foot of the horse is made of one toe with a strong, hard hoof. The rear of the foot has a tough, elastic pad which acts like a rubber heel in absorbing shocks.

The mare has a gestation period of about 11 months, after which she gives birth to one colt (baby horse). The colt is able to walk and run a few hours after birth. It is full-grown by the time it is five years old. Stallions usually start mating when they are two years old, mares when they are three or four. Most mares will bear six colts during their lifetime, but some may bear as many as 19. Horses usually live for about 30 years.

Horses are herbivores and eat grass by biting it off near the ground. Horses have been

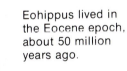
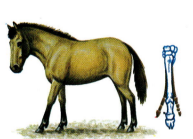

The modern horse, below, differs greatly from its ancestors, two of which are shown at the right. Note the difference in foot structure.

Eohippus lived in the Eocene epoch, about 50 million years ago.

Merychippus lived in the Miocene epoch, about 20 million years ago.

domesticated for thousands of years, and have been used for many purposes. The only truly wild horse still in existance is Przewalski's horse, a stocky, light brown animal living in small numbers on the plains of central Asia. The other so-called wild horses of today are actually domestic horses which escaped and started to live in the wild again. The number of these "wild horses," or mustangs, in the United States has dropped from several million in the 1800s to fewer than 20,000 today. For this reason, federal laws were established in 1971 to protect them from hunters.

A.J.C./J.J.M.

HORSE CHESTNUT (hòrs ches' net)
The horse chestnut is a tree that originally came from Asia and is now found throughout the United States. It is planted as an ornamental tree because it provides good shade and has a very lovely flower. The flowers are pink or white. They grow in conical clusters. Large nuts grow inside a green, spiny case. The tree is called a chestnut because the nut of the tree resembles the nut of the American chestnut. However, the two trees are not closely related. The horse chestnut tree grows to 24 m [80 ft] in height. *See also* CHESTNUT.

S.R.G./M.H.S.

HORSEFLY (hòrs' flī') The horsefly is any of several species of stout-bodied flies with

Front view of the head of a horsefly, showing its mouth parts and the brilliantly-colored eyes.

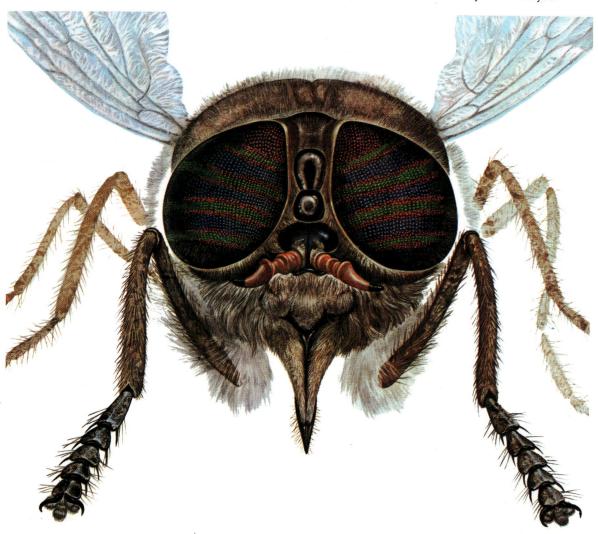

large, brilliantly colored compound eyes. (*See* EYE AND VISION.) The female bites human beings, horses, and other animals. After making the bite with the sharp mouthparts, she inserts a tubelike proboscis through which she sucks blood. Male horseflies usually feed on nectar and do not bite animals. Larvae develop from eggs which are usually laid near brooks or streams. The larvae eat earthworms and other small, soft animals.

The most common horsefly (*Tabanas atratus*) has a black body. Horseflies may carry disease-causing parasites and bacteria. The horsefly is sometimes called the gadfly. *See also* FLY. A.J.C./J.E.R.

HORSEHEAD NEBULA (hòrs' hed neb' yə lə) The Horsehead nebula is a dark cloud of gas and dust located in the constellation Orion. When viewed through a telescope, the Horsehead nebula has a greenish glow. The Horsehead nebula is so named because it resembles the shape of a horse's head. We can see this nebula because there is a bright nebula behind it, and the horsehead shape blocks the light from the bright nebula. *See also* NEBULA. J.M.C./C.R.

HORSEPOWER (hòr' spaùr') Horsepower is a unit of power used in the foot-pound-second system of units. (*See* FOOT-POUND-SECOND SYSTEM.) If you move a weight upwards, you are doing work against gravity. If you push a car along a level road, you are doing work against friction. Power is the rate at which work is done. Originally, one horsepower was reckoned to be the power of one horse. It was used to describe early steam engines. If a steam engine had a horsepower of two, then it could do the work of two horses. In the foot-pound-second system, one horsepower is equal to 550 foot-pounds per second. In the SI system of units, it is equal to 746 watts. (*See* INTERNATIONAL SYSTEM.)

For an automobile engine, the horsepower can be calculated from the rate of work of the pistons. This is called the indicated horsepower. Some of this power is used to overcome friction inside the engine. The rest of the indicated horsepower drives the automobile. This is called the brake horsepower. M.E./R.W.L.

HORSERADISH (hòrs' rad' ish) Horseradish (*Armoracia rusticana*) is a perennial, herbaceous plant belonging to the mustard family. It is native to Europe. It has long, toothed leaves growing from large roots. Clusters of small, white flowers grow along stems which are about 60 cm [2 ft] tall. The roots are grated for use in making the bitter, sharp-tasting relish which is also known as horseradish. *See also* MUSTARD FAMILY. A.J.C./F.W.S.

These horsetails grow in damp places in the northern temperate zones. They are living fossils.

HORSETAIL (hòr' stāl') The horsetail is any of 20 species of primitive land plants belonging to the genus *Equisetum*. Horsetails are distantly related to ferns and club mosses. They grow in damp places in temperate and tropical areas. They are usually small and treelike, except they have hollow stems. Horsetails grow from perennial rhizomes. (*See* RHIZOME).

Horsetails do not produce flowers. Instead they produce reproductive stalks with cone-like structures containing spores. (*See* ASEXUAL REPRODUCTION.) Horsetails contain silica and were once used for polishing metal. This led to their nickname, scouring rush.

Horsetails are the sole survivors of an important group of plants of the Carboniferous period when some species grew as large as trees. Their remains form an important part of coal.   A.J.C./M.H.S.

The horsetail has no roots. It grows from an underground rhizome. A vegetative shoot is at the right. The fertile stem at the left bears a "cone" containing spores.

HORTICULTURE (hör′ tə kəl′ chər) Horticulture is a branch of agriculture that specializes in increasing the quality and quantity of fruits, vegetables, flowers, trees, and shrubs. Horticulturalists try to determine the best growing conditions for plants— including type of soil, types and amounts of fertilizers, methods of cultivation, and methods of insect, weed, and disease control.

Horticulture has led to the development of new, stronger, more productive varieties of plants. They have made it possible for farmers to produce more high quality food on less land. *See also* AGRICULTURE; BOTANY.
                A.J.C./F.W.S.

HOUSEFLY (haùs′ flī′) The housefly (*Musca domestica*) is one of the most widely distributed of all insects. It is a major pest and health hazard, particularly in parts of the world where sanitary conditions are poor. The housefly has a dull gray, bristled body that is about 7 mm [0.3 in] long. It has large, reddish compound eyes. (*See* EYE AND VISION.) Its mouth cannot bite, but consists of a spongy pad. The housefly eats by oozing saliva and digestive juices over food and then sponging up the resulting solution. In this way, houseflies contaminate large amounts of food. Houseflies often carry one or more disease-causing microorganisms in their saliva or on their bodies and legs.

Houseflies usually live and breed in or near garbage or organic wastes (such as feces). The female lays about 100 eggs at a time and as many as 1,000 during her lifetime. The eggs hatch into larvae, or maggots, in 12 to 30 hours. The maggots molt several times before becoming pupae. (*See* MOLTING.) Within a few days, the pupae become adults and the cycle begins again. (*See* METAMORPHOSIS.) Most adult houseflies live for about 30 days in the summer, longer when the weather is cooler. Cold weather usually

A housefly feeding on meat is shown above. The fly pours saliva and other digestive juices on the meat and mops up the mixture with its spongy mouth—spreading germs as it does so.

kills off the adults, but larvae and pupae are able to survive the winter. *See also* FLY.
A.J.C./J.E.R.

HOVERCRAFT *See* AIR-CUSHION VEHICLE.

HOWLER MONKEY (hau′ lər məng′ kē) The howler monkey is any of five species of monkeys belonging to genus *Alouatta* of the family Cebidae. They are the largest in this family, often growing to a height of 60 cm [2 ft] with tails at least that long. They weigh about 8 kg [17.6 lb] and have red, black, or brown fur. Howler monkeys live in tropical forests in South America.

The howler monkey gets its name from its deafening, howling roar. Its howl is so loud that it can be heard more than 3 km [1.8 mi] away. The sounds are made by a large, bony resonating chamber in the throat. This chamber produces an obvious swelling under the chin. Howler monkeys howl when they wake up in the morning and when disturbed

The howler monkey gets its name from its unpleasantly loud voice.

by noise or approaching rain. They also howl to warn off intruders in their territory. Howler monkeys live in trees, sometimes hanging by their tails while feeding on leaves and fruits. (*See* HERBIVORE.) These mammals usually travel in groups of 15 to 20. *See also* MONKEY; RESONANCE. A.J.C./J.J.M.

HOYLE, SIR FRED (1915–   ) Sir Fred Hoyle (hoil) is a British astronomer. He is famous for his work on the origin of the universe. Hoyle suggested that new matter is being made in the universe all the time. But this idea is not now generally accepted. Hoyle has found that heavy elements can be formed inside stars. Stars change their nature as they get older. Hoyle has studied the way they change.

Hoyle has other interesting theories about physics. He has suggested that gravity might not always stay the same. This means that things could change in weight after a long time. His study of quasars had made him believe that our knowledge of physics is not great enough to understand them. He is also famous for his science-fiction stories. (*See* QUASARS.) C.M./D.G.F.

HUBBLE, EDWIN POWELL (1889–1953) Edwin Hubble (həb′ əl) was a famous American astronomer. He was interested in nebulae and galaxies.

He worked at the Mount Wilson Observatory, with its famous 100-inch telescope (the largest in the world at that time). He used this telescope to find stars that were outside our own galaxy. He helped to show that there are other galaxies outside our own. In 1929, he showed that these galaxies are all moving apart at enormous speeds. This is called the theory of the expanding universe. Some scientists believe that all the matter of the stars was once concentrated in one very dense lump. Then this lump exploded and all the fragments became the stars. The stars are moving apart like bits of an exploding bomb.

Hubble calculated how long ago this explosion was. He believed it was about 10 billion years ago. The ratio of speed to distance for galaxies is called the Hubble constant. *See also* COSMOLOGY; RED SHIFT.   C.M./D.G.F.

HUMAN BEING

Human beings (hyü′ mən bē′ ings) are unique animals. No other animals live in all climates, create fire, pray, or destroy their own kind in wars. Because they are such complicated animals, human beings are studied in a number of different ways.

The brain of human beings is highly developed. This results in the ability to think, work out problems, and form ideas. A combination of this unique brain and a highly developed voice enables human beings to speak. They therefore communicate their ideas to others. The skill with which human beings can use their hands is also unique. Using this skill, they can use tools, write, and create art—again allowing them to communicate ideas and to record them. All art, religion, science, literature, civilization, and culture are the results of such abilities.

Human beings are the only creatures to study themselves and their achievements. Anatomy studies the structure of the human body. Physiology is the study of how the body works. Through psychology, the human mind is explored. Sociology is the study of how people behave in groups. Anthropology includes the study of the differences between the various human races and cultures. Human beings study the nature and workings of the world around them through many branches of science, such as astronomy, biology, chemistry, geology, and physics. These studies, and many more, help people to understand themselves, to conquer diseases, and to plan for the future. Such studies have enabled people to survive in various surroundings. By developing agriculture, engineering, and medicine, people have been able to use and control many aspects of the environment to their advantage. Yet human beings are also the most destructive of creatures. Besides the capacity to destroy themselves and all other life, they have the ability to change the balance of nature. They create pollution and misuse pesticides that kill wildlife.

Scientific classification   Within the animal kingdom, scientists place human beings in the subkingdom Metazoa. Metazoa includes all living things made up of many cells and having true digestive cavities. Human beings belong to the phylum Chordata. Chordata includes all creatures with a nerve cord and a notochord along the back. The human backbone puts human beings in the subphylum Vertebrata. Vertebrates form several classes, among them Mammalia, to which the human being belongs. Nearly all mammals give birth to live young and nurse them with milk.

The more than 4,000 species of mammals make up 19 orders. Scientists place human beings, apes, monkeys, lemurs, and tarsiers in the order Primates. Primates have well-developed control over their fingers and toes, and can grasp objects easily. Most primates have excellent eyesight and stereoscopic vision. Stereoscopic vision allows them to judge depth. Human beings, monkeys, and apes make up the suborder Anthropoidea. People and apes alone form the superfamily Hominoidea. The family of human beings, the Hominidae, includes human beings of prehistoric times as well as all modern human races. Some scientists divide this family into two groups, genus *Australopithecus* and genus *Homo*. Other scientists divide the family Hominidae into several different species. Scientists agree that all living human beings today are genus *Homo,* species *sapiens.* *Homo sapiens* are latin words that mean "wise man."

The development of the human being Human beings and the apes have developed from the same primate ancestor. This ancestor is now extinct. The most important differences between apes and human beings are brain size and the ability to walk upright. *Ramepithecus,* an ape that lived about 12 million years ago, showed some human characteristics. However, true humanlike fossils do not occur until much later. Until recently the oldest humanlike fossil known was *Australopithecus.* But in 1972, Dr. Richard Leakey discovered a fossil skull in Kenya. This skull had a much larger brain then *Australopithecus.* This fossil is about 2.5 million years old. It could possibly represent the "missing link" between apes and human beings.

More recent fossils, dating from about 750,000 years ago, show definite relationships to human beings. *Pithecanthropus* was very humanlike. But *Pithecanthropus* had prominent ridges over the eyes and some apelike features. Other remains dating from that time are generally classified under *Homo erectus.* Examples are the Java man and Peking man. All fossils of *Homo erectus* are at least 400,000 years old. From this creature, several types of the human beings seem to have developed. One was the Neanderthal. The Neanderthal looked very primitive with thick, stocky body and enlarged eyebrow ridges. However, the Neanderthal possessed a large brain. The Neanderthals also used various stone tools and buried their dead. They lived in Europe until about 35,000 years ago, when human beings like ourselves replaced them.

The change came too quickly for the modern human being to have descended from the Neanderthals. The modern human being probably evolved separately, directly from *Homo erectus.* Some of the earliest known remains of *Homo sapiens,* such as the Steinheim man and the Swanscombe man, are more than 100,000 years old. Among the most famous prehistoric humans are those found in France at Cro-Magnon and elsewhere. They lived in caves. The caves were decorated with drawings.

Races of human beings All modern human beings are placed in the same biological species, *Homo sapiens.* Many people have suggested that human beings be divided into five main races. They are Caucasoid, meaning "white skinned," Negroid, meaning "black skinned," Mongoloid, meaning "yellow skinned," Australoid (the Australian aborigines), and Capoid (the Bushmen of South Africa). Other anthropologists, people who study human groups, reject racial classifications. But anthropologists nevertheless study the relationships between groups living in various parts of the world (*See* ANTHROPOLOGY.)

Because of all their mental and physical abilities, human beings have come to dominate most other living things. They have adapted themselves to their surroundings. They have also adapted nature to their needs. People have built machines that carry them around the world. They have built cities that hold millions of people. They have split atoms, shot rockets into space, and spun satellites around the earth.

Although human beings may harness nature, they are not free from the laws that govern all living things. People have slowly come to realize that they must work to conserve the earth's natural resources. Only in this way will future generations be able to carry on the way of life that they have created.

For thousands of years, human beings have searched for spiritual essences, or values that give meaning to life. Their sense of beauty is communicated in works of art. This creates an international language. Philosophy shows the human need for truth. Indeed, it is this unique quality of imagination, of thinking beyond the world around him, that has placed human beings, for better or worse, where they are. J.J.A./J.J.M.

HUMBOLDT, BARON ALEXANDER VON (1769–1859)

Baron Alexander von Humboldt (hùm' bōlt) was a German scientist and explorer. He is famous for his travels in South America, Europe, and Asia. He used the information that he collected on his travels to add to knowledge in many fields. Humboldt drew the first isothermal map. This showed the different climates of different places. He also linked this information with the types of plants that grew in different places. He studied volcanoes and sea currents. The cold current that flows north from the West coast of South America is named after him.

Humboldt turned his five-year journey around South America (1799–1804) into a book. The book took 20 years to write. It was full of new information about biology, astronomy, and geology. His last book was called *Kosmos*. In this book, Humboldt tried to show the way everything in the universe fits together. C.M./D.G.F.

HUMERUS

(hyüm' rəs) The humerus is a large bone in the upper half of the arm. The humerus lies between the shoulder and the elbow. The upper part of the bone has a ball-shaped head. This head fits into a cup-shaped hollow or socket in a large bone in the back called the shoulder blade.

The head of the humerus can move around quite freely in its socket. This allows the arm to move in many directions. J.A./J.J.F.

HUMIDITY

(hyü mid' ət ē) Humidity is the amount of water vapor in the air. It is always changing, because the warmer the air is, the more water vapor it can hold. Absolute humidity measures the amount of water vapor in a given volume of air.

At any given temperature, the air can only hold a certain amount of water vapor. If the air is holding as much water vapor as it possibly can, the air is said to be saturated. When this happens, the temperature is equal to the dew point, and some of the water vapor condenses out of the air in the form of dew or fog. (*See* CONDENSATION.)

Relative humidity is the amount of water vapor in the air compared to the amount needed for saturation. When the air is saturated, the relative humidity equals 100%. If the air is holding half as much water vapor as it possibly can, the relative humidity equals 50%.

Meteorologists measure relative humidity with an instrument called a hygrometer. Humidity has a significant effect on comfort, especially on hot days. On a hot day with high humidity, most people feel sticky because perspiration does not evaporate off their bodies. (*See* EVAPORATION.) The very low humidity associated with bitter cold winter weather gives people a biting sensation in the winter air. *See also* METEOROLOGY.

J.M.C./C.R.

HUMMINGBIRD

(həm' ing' bərd) A hummingbird is a very small bird that belongs to the family Trochilidae. There are 15 species found in North America. Fourteen species are found only in the western and southwestern part of North America. Only the ruby-throated hummingbird is found east of the Mississippi River. Hummingbirds are the smallest of all North American birds. The smallest, the Calliope hummingbird, is only 7.5 cm [2.75 in] long. The largest, the blue-throated hummingbird, is 13.1 cm [5.25 in] long. Most species are about 6.8 cm [3 in] long. Hummingbirds are so named because

Hummingbirds feed mainly on nectar. They hover in front of blossoms and plunge their long beak into the nectar.

their wings beat so fast they make a humming sound. They can hover in midair and even fly backwards. Hummingbirds have a high metabolism. (*See* METABOLISM.) They require large amounts of food to survive. The birds eat sugar-rich nectar which they suck out of flowers with their long, slender bills and tongues.   S.R.G./L.L.S.

HUMUS (hyü′ məs) Humus is the dark, rich part of soil. It comes from dead plants and animals. The plants and animals die, fall to the ground, and slowly rot and are mixed into

Humus is a valuable component of soil. Humus is formed from decayed plant and animal materials. Leaves add to humus.

the dirt. This process returns the nutrients back to the soil where they came from. (*See* NUTRITION.) A sandy beach has no humus. The soil in a forest has a lot of humus. The leaves from the trees that die and fall to the ground help to build up humus. Humus allows plants to grow better.   S.R.G./R.J.B.

HURRICANE (hər′ ə kān′) A hurricane is a violent tropical cyclone, with winds of at least 120 km [75 mi] per hour. Tropical cyclones are named according to where they form. A hurricane forms in the western North Atlantic Ocean, a typhoon in the west Pacific, a cyclone in the Indian Ocean, and a willy-willy near Australia.

Hurricane formation   There are several requirements for hurricane formation. They can only develop over ocean waters of at least 27°C [80°F]. The area of formation must be at least 5° latitude away from the equator. At the equator there is no Coriolis force. The Coriolis force is needed to produce cyclonic wind circulation. Cyclonic winds are counterclockwise in the northern hemisphere, clockwise in the southern hemisphere. If the first two requirements for creating a hurricane are met, a large mass of thunderstorms can combine to form a common updraft, thus creating an area of low atmospheric pressure. Winds begin to revolve in a cyclonic direction around the low pressure area. At the same time, water is being evaporated and condensed, pumping energy into the system.

There are three stages in the formation of a hurricane. Tropical depression is the stage where the storm is rather undefined but appears to be strengthening. When the depression gains more power, it is called a tropical storm. When the wind speed reaches 120 km [75 mi] per hour, it is called a hurricane.

Hurricane structure The center of the hurricane is a calm area called the eye. This area of lowest atmospheric pressure measures about 5 to 15 km [3 to 5 mi] in diameter. In the eye, the weather is calm and the skies may be clear. Surrounding the eye is a doughnut-shaped area called the anulus. In the anulus exists the most violent weather of the hurricane. Huge cumulonimbus clouds form a wall around the eye. (*See* CLOUD.) Severe thunderstorms and winds of 209 to 241 km [130 to 150 mi] per hour have been recorded. Surrounding the anulus is a large spiral-shaped area of rain and scattered thunderstorms. The full diameter of a mature hurricane is usually from 480 to 960 km [300 to 600 mi], and sometimes larger. The clouds may reach 5.5 km [18,000 ft] into the atmosphere.

Hurricane movement and destruction Hurricanes usually move westward at first, but then shift to north or northeast. This movement makes the Gulf of Mexico coast and the eastern United States particularly vulnerable to a hurricane.

Hurricanes are usually preceded by a storm surge. Storm surges are great waves that may cause extensive damage to coastal areas. As the hurricane moves over land, strong winds and rain increase in intensity until the eye arrives. There may be an hour of calm winds and no precipitation. But when the eye moves on, the full fury of the storm returns.

Hurricanes rapidly lose energy after they reach land. This happens because the moisture source is cut off, and because of friction between the storm and the land. If a hurricane gets far enough north, it may cross a front, and be transformed into a regular storm.

The National Weather Service watches all hurricane activity, and informs the public of any important developments. If a hurricane threatens a land area, a hurricane warning is issued. This means that the population of that area must take the necessary precautions to avoid damage and casualties. *See also* METEOROLOGY. J.M.C./C.R.

Hurricane Gladys was photographed from the United States Apollo 7 spacecraft in 1968.

HUTTON, JAMES (1726–1797) James Hutton (hət′ ən) was a Scottish geologist. He began by studying medicine, then became a farmer. Through farming and studying chemistry, he became interested in geology. This was not a real science when Hutton started work. His most important idea was that geological changes are continuously going on. Until then, scientists had believed that the earth changed in sudden bursts, which they called catastrophes.   C.M./D.G.F.

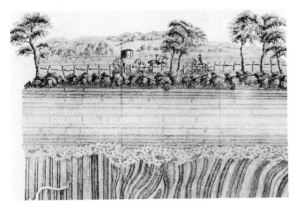

Illustration in James Hutton's *Theory of the Earth.*

HUYGENS, CHRISTIAN (1629–1695) Christian Huygens (hȯi′ gəns) was a Dutch scientist. He studied mathematics, physics, and astronomy. He was interested in light and made what was then the biggest telescope in the world. He found one of the moons of Saturn with this telescope, and saw the planet's rings. He invented the first pendulum clock in 1657. Huygens' most famous work is the discovery of polarized light. He also developed the wave theory of light. *See also* LIGHT; POLARIZED LIGHT.   C.M./D.G.F.

HUYGENS' PRINCIPLE (hȯi′ gəns prin′ spəl) Huygens' principle helps us understand how waves behave. It was first proposed by Christian Huygens, a Dutch scientist. It states that each point in a wave can be thought of as the source of more waves. For example, suppose that sound is entering a room through an open door. Huygens' principle says that, in

effect, the doorway is the source of the sound. The waves reaching you behave as if this were so.

Huygens' principle is very useful in the study of light. It is used to work out problems in diffraction and interference. (*See* DIFFRACTION; INTERFERENCE.) For example, if light passes through a narrow slit, the light is diffracted. This causes it to spread out. The slit can be regarded as the source of light. This allows the spreading of the light to be more easily understood.   M.E./S.S.B.

HYACINTH (hī′ ə sinth) The hyacinth is a spring flower of the lily family Liliaceae. Its bell-shaped flowers of blue, pink, white, yellow, or purple, bloom in March and April on stalks that grow from 15 to 46 cm [6 to 18 in] high. Hyacinths grow from bulbs in open beds, hothouses, and in the home.

The hyacinth originated in Asia and Africa, and was brought to Europe in the early 1500s. Today, it is a popular plant in many parts of the world. The soil and climate of the Netherlands provide a particularly favorable place for growing hyacinths. The Dutch plant a large number every year near Haarlem, Holland. They ship the bulbs to many parts of the world, including the United States.

Hyacinths raised in open beds need rich, well-drained soil. The bulbs are planted between September and November, and flowers appear in the early spring. Gardeners usually tie the stems to stakes for added support. In summer the bulbs are dug and stored after the leaves have withered.   W.R.P./M.H.S.

HYATT, JOHN WESLEY (1837–1920) John Hyatt (hī′ ət) was an American printer who invented many different things. He worked out a way of purifying a large amount of water. He also invented a roller bearing that is still used in modern machinery. His most interesting work was in the use of cellulose. He read that a prize was to be given for the best idea for making a synthetic billiard ball. Billiard balls then were made of ivory, which was very rare and expensive. Hyatt made a mixture of nitrocellulose, camphor, and alcohol. This could be molded under pressure when it was gently warmed. He won the prize and patented his invention in 1870. He also worked out a way of making thin sheets of celluloid good enough to use for photography. Hyatt's work with cellulose made him one of the pioneers of the plastics industry. *See also* PLASTIC; PHOTOGRAPHY.

C.M./D.G.F.

HYBRID (hī′ brəd) A hybrid is the offspring of two parents that belong to different species, stock, breeds, or races. The mule is an example of a hybrid animal. Its parents are a jackass (male donkey) and a mare (female horse). The parents of some hybrids differ only slightly. Hybrid plants, such as corn, are produced by plants that differ in only a few traits. If the parents of a hybrid are very different, the hybrid may be sterile (unable to reproduce). The mule is one of those kinds of hybrids.

Hybrids occur naturally, and some are created by man's actions. Sometimes, in the case of natural hybrids, new species are created that are better able to handle their surroundings than their parents. Each parent of a hybrid has a different set of genes, and these genes are passed on to the offspring during reproduction. Some hybrids, particularly dogs, are called mongrels.

New plants can be developed through hybridization. The best hybrids may be superior to the parents in hardiness, yield, and resistance to disease. The cultivated strawberry is a good example. It has larger fruit and better flavor than its wild parents. Some hybrid tomatoes contain more vitamins than either parent. Hybrid corn produces higher yields, and withstands disease and drought better than regular varieties.

Hybridization in plants was developed in the early 1900s when scientists developed breeding methods based on Gregor Mendel's theories of plant heredity.

Hybridization in animals is more difficult than hybridization in plants. Plant crosses are easier to control than animal crosses. The cattalo is an example of a successful hybrid animal. The cattalo is a cross between domestic cattle and the American buffalo. Cattle breeders have also successfully crossed Brahman cattle of India with Afrikanders cattle of Africa. This hybrid endures the heat and humidity of the tropics, and resists diseases better than its parents and other varieties. Hybrid fowl, like chicken and turkeys, have been developed to produce more white meat on their breasts.

Animal hybridization is limited. Many animals are unable to mate because their genes do not react correctly. *See also* BURBANK, LUTHER; MENDEL, GREGOR.

W.R.P./M.H.S.

HYDRA (hī′ drə) The hydra is one of the simplest multicellular animals and is one of the very few members of the phylum Cnidaria that lives in fresh water. (*See* CNIDARIA.) The largest hydras are only about 15 mm [0.6 in] long. The body of the hydra is called a polyp. Polyps are tube-shaped and sessile, meaning they usually stay in one place. The hydra attaches to underwater plants by means of a tiny pedal disk. It sometimes moves by sliding along on this pedal disk or by somersaulting through the water.

The hydra has a mouth opening at the unattached end of its body. The mouth is surrounded by five or six tentacles which are used to capture insect larvae and tiny water animals. Prey are paralyzed by a poison injected through nematocysts, tiny stinging threads in the tentacles. The hydra is said to have an incomplete digestive system because food enters and wastes leave through the same opening.

Hydras usually reproduce by budding,

each bud becoming a new organism. (*See* ASEXUAL REPRODUCTION; BUDDING.) In cool weather, however, hydras reproduce sexually. The hydra forms sperms and eggs which join within its body to form embryos. (*See* HERMAPHRODITE.) These embryos develop tough coats which protect them from drying or temperature changes. This is probably an adaptation to allow hydras to survive in areas where their habitat (ponds or lakes) dry up for part of the year.

Hydras can regenerate lost parts and, in fact, regenerate all their body cells every few weeks. (*See* REGENERATION.)

The most common hydras are the green hydra (*Chlorohydra viridissima*) and the brown hydra (*Pelmatohydra oligactis*). They get their color from algae which live symbiotically within the inner layer of cells of the hydras. (*See* SYMBIOSIS.)   A.J.C./C.S.H.

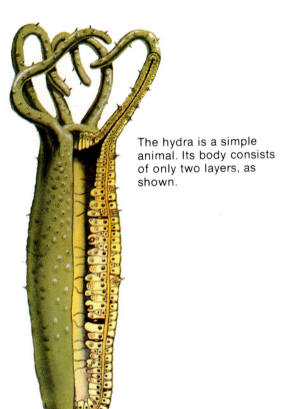

The hydra is a simple animal. Its body consists of only two layers, as shown.

HYDRANGEA (hī drān' jə) The hydrangea is a genus of handsome, flowering shrubs in the Hydrangeaceae family. One species grows 9 m [30 ft] high. A dwarf variety grows to about 3.7 m [12 ft]. The flowers are white, pink, or bluish, and grow in large, showy clusters. Each individual flower has 4 or 5 petals. Hydrangeas grow best in rich, slightly moist soil and in partially shaded areas. They bloom from late summer until fall. Hydrangeas are found in North and South America, China, and Japan.

Pink hydrangeas produce blue flowers when grown in soil treated with aluminum sulfate, or alum. Lime added to the soil makes blue hydrangeas produce pink flowers. Hydrangeas are grown by planting either cuttings or seeds.   W.R.P./M.H.S.

HYDRATE (hī' drāt) A hydrate is a compound that forms crystals containing water. The water molecules are linked to the molecules of the compound. The water is called water of crystallization. The number of molecules of water can be shown in the chemical formula. For example, the formula for sodium carbonate is Na_2CO_3. When it forms a hydrate, it takes up ten molecules of water. The formula is now $Na_2CO_3 \cdot 10\ H_2O$.

The salts of some metals form more than one hydrate. Copper sulfate forms at least three. They can be written $CuSO_4 \cdot H_2O$, $CuSO_4 \cdot 3H_2O$, and $CuSO_4 \cdot 5H_2O$. Copper sulfate in the form of its hydrate makes deep blue crystals. If it is heated, the water of crystallization evaporates. The blue color disappears. White powder is left, containing no water. This is copper sulfate in its anhydrous state. Anhydrous means without water. When water is added, the blue color returns.

Some hydrates lose their water without heating. When the air is dry, their crystals become white and powdery. This is called efflorescence. Cobalt chloride shows a color change when it gains water. When it is a hydrate it forms pink crystals. It is blue when it is anhydrous. It can be used to show whether there is moisture inside a container or not. The blue crystals become pink if moisture is present. D.M.H.W./A.D.

HYDRAULICS (hī drȯ′ liks) Hydraulics is the study of the use of water and other liquids in engineering. The name comes from the ancient Greek word *hydraulis*. A hydraulis was a musical instrument. The pressure of water in pipes was used to regulate the flow of air in the instrument. Today we use the pressure of liquids to work all kinds of machines and devices.

Water and other liquids cannot be compressed. It is this property that is so useful in hydraulics. Liquids flow because their molecules can easily move past each other. But the molecules cannot be squeezed any closer together. Pressure in a liquid is transmitted in every direction. If liquid is enclosed in a tube, force can be transmitted instantaneously from one end to the other. Most hydraulic devices

consist of a tube joining two sealed containers of liquid. A sealed system like this is called a hydraulic system.

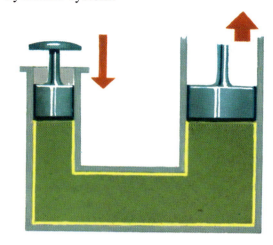

Above: Diagram of the principle of the hydraulic jack. Pressure exerted on the small piston raises the larger piston. Below: diagram of the hydraulic lift system of a tractor. Oil pumped through the narrow transfer pipe enters the wide ram cylinder and pushes the ram piston backward. This raises the lift arms.

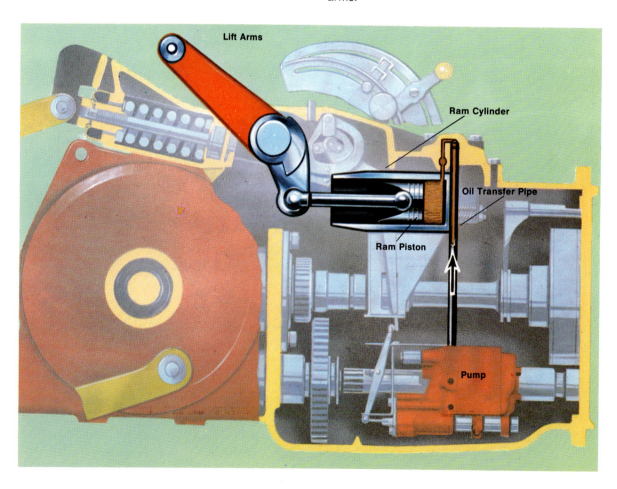

In a hydraulic system, each chamber is a hollow cylinder. Inside is a movable piston. The piston fits tightly, sealing it. When one poston moves in, the pressure forces liquid along the tube. The other piston is forced outwards by the pressure.

Automobile brakes and clutches are worked by hydraulics. They work instantly and smoothly. There are many other machines that have hydraulic systems. Airplanes rely on them to operate their control surfaces. Ailerons, flaps, elevators, and rudders are all worked by hydraulics, and so is the landing gear. Barber's and dentist's chairs are raised and lowered by hydraulics. The same principle is used in some hand jacks for automobiles. Heavy equipment for forging and stamping metals relies on the tremendous force that can be applied.

Applied hydraulics is the branch of engineering that deals with the uses of hydraulics in industry. Electricity generators, pumps, and water supply systems rely on the flow of water. The behavior of flowing water and other liquids is studied in fluid mechanics. The hydraulic ram is a pump. It uses water pressure to pump quantities of water to a greater height. This is one way of storing energy. The higher the water is, the more power there is available.   D.M.H.W./J.D.

HYDRAZINE (hī′ drə zēn′) Hydrazine (N_2H_4) is a colorless liquid with an unpleasant odor resembling that of ammonia. Hydrazine boils at 113.5°C [236.3°F] and it freezes at 1.4°C [34.5°F]. It is a flammable liquid and is used as a fuel in rocket and jet engines. Hydrazine is sometimes added to water in boilers. It helps to prevent rust forming on the inside of the boiler.   M.E./J.M.

HYDRIDE (hī′ drīd) A hydride is a compound of an element with hydrogen. Hydrides may be made by directly combining the element with hydrogen gas. Sometimes a catalyst is needed to make the reaction work.

Hydrides may also be formed by using reducing agents. (*See* OXIDATION AND REDUCTION.) A reducing agent is a chemical compound that supplies atoms of hydrogen. When a compound accepts hydrogen in a reaction, it is said to be reduced.

There are several kinds of hydrides. Sodium, potassium, and lithium are elements high in the electromotive series. They combine with hydrogen to give sodium hydride, potassium hydride, and lithium hydride. These readily give up their hydrogen in chemical reactions. They are good reducing agents. Lithium aluminum hydride ($LiAlH_4$) is a particularly strong reducing agent.

Elements low in the electromotive series also combine with hydrogen. The halogens are examples. With chlorine, hydrogen forms hydrogen chloride. It could also be thought of as chlorine hydride. In the same way, bromine hydride is more usually called hydrogen bromide. These compounds dissolve in water to form strong acids.

Nonmetals such as nitrogen and phosphorus also combine with hydrogen. Again, the compounds are not normally called hydrides. With nitrogen, hydrogen forms ammonia (NH_3). With phosphorus it forms phosphine (PH_3). With carbon, hydrogen forms a huge number of different compounds. They are called the hydrocarbons.

Palladium forms hydrides with large quantities of hydrogen. This also happens with some other transition metals. These may not be true compounds, however. They may be mixtures of elements with hydrogen. They are rather like alloys.   D.M.H.W./A.D.

HYDROCARBONS (hī′ drə kär′ bənz) Hydrocarbons are important compounds of carbon and hydrogen. Because they contain carbon, they are organic compounds. They are found naturally in coal and oil and as gases under the earth. Gasoline, kerosene and candle wax all consist of hydrocarbons. Many hydrocarbons are valuable as fuels. There are two kinds of compounds that carbon and hydrogen can form. They are called the aliphatic compounds and the aromatic compounds.

Aliphatic hydrocarbons In aliphatic hydrocarbons, the carbon atoms are linked together in short or long chains or, sometimes, in rings. The chains may be straight or have branches to the sides. Carbon has a valence of four. This means that each atom can link with four other atoms. It is possible to make a huge molecule by linking carbon atom after carbon atom together. Hydrogen atoms are attached to the sides of the chain. Each hydrogen atom forms a link, or bond, with one carbon atom. A carbon atom may have a single bond with another carbon atom, or a double bond, or even a triple bond.

The simplest hydrocarbon of all is methane. This has one carbon surrounded by four atoms of hydrogen. Its formula is CH_4. Methane is marsh gas. It is found in natural gases. Ethane is another gas. It has two carbon atoms joined together by a single bond. All the other bonds are with hydrogen atoms. The formula for ethane is C_2H_6. Propane is C_3H_8, and butane is C_4H_{10}. Octane has eight carbon atoms linked together. Its formula is C_8H_{18}. Octane is important in gasoline. This series of compounds is called the alkane, or paraffin, series.

The series of compounds that has two carbon atoms joined by double bonds is called the alkene or olefin series. (*See* OLEFIN.) The simplest alkene is ethylene. Its formula can be written $CH_2{=}CH_2$. Ethylene is used to make the plastic polyethylene by polymerization. Compounds with more than one double bond are called alkadienes or diolefins. An example is butadiene, $CH_2{=}CH{-}CH{=}CH_2$. Butadiene is used to make synthetic rubber. Alkynes have one triple bond. Acetylene is an example. Its formula is $CH{\equiv}CH$. The alkanes are all saturated compounds. This means that they have the maximum number of

hydrogen atoms in each molecule. They have no double or triple bonds. The alkenes, diolefins and alkynes do not have the maximum number of hydrogen atoms in each molecule. They have double or triple bonds between carbon atoms. They are unsaturated.

Cyclic aliphatic hydrocarbons Some aliphatic compounds consist of carbon atoms arranged in rings. If the rings consist only of carbon atoms, they are called alicyclic compounds. Cyclohexane (C_6H_{12}) is an example. It has six $-CH_2-$ groups joined together by single bonds. Compounds containing rings of carbon atoms with one or more other kinds of atoms joined into the ring are called heterocyclic compounds.

Aromatic hydrocarbons Aromatic hydrocarbons have a special type of ring structure. They are called aromatic because they have a strong smell. Aromatics are based on the structure of benzene (C_6H_6). Benzene consists of six carbon atoms forming a ring. Each carbon atom is linked on one side by a double bond to a neighboring carbon atom and by a single bond on the other side. Naphthalene consists of two benzene rings linked together.

Substituted hydrocarbons Both aliphatic and aromatic hydrocarbons form more complicated compounds. This happens when hydrogen atoms in the hydrocarbons are replaced by other atoms or, in some cases, by chains of atoms. For example, chloroform, the anesthetic, consists of methane in which three of the hydrogen atoms have been replaced by chlorine atoms - $CHCl_3$. Aromatic hydrocarbons also form substituted compounds in the same way. For example, phenol (C_6H_5OH) consists of a benzene ring in which one hydrogen atom has been replaced by an -OH group. Sometimes an aromatic compound has an aliphatic chain attached to it.

M.E./A.I.

HYDROCHLORIC ACID (hī′ drə klōr′ ik as′ əd) Hydrochloric acid is a strong acid. It is made by dissolving hydrogen chloride gas in water. Its formula is HCl. Concentrated hydrochloric acid contains 39% hydrogen chloride. It is a colorless liquid when it is absolutely pure. It usually has a yellowish color when there are impurities. The acid is very poisonous and dangerous. It is extremely corrosive. It burns holes in clothes and eats into metal. It gives off fumes in moist air. It must be handled very carefully.

When hydrochloric acid reacts with many metals, bubbles are given off. Hydrogen gas is produced. At the same time the salt of the acid is formed. The salts of hydrochloric acid are called chlorides. Chlorides are also formed when hydrochloric acid reacts with bases.

Hydrochloric acid can be manufactured by bubbling hydrogen chloride gas through water. Another method is to add concentrated sulfuric acid to sodium chloride (common salt). Chlorine gas also produces hydrochloric acid when it reacts with certain hydrocarbons.

Hydrochloric acid is used to produce other chemicals. It is used to make dyes and to produce textiles and leather goods. It is also used in the manufacture of glues and glucose. In many industries it is used to clean metal surfaces. In the automobile industry it is used to remove rust and dirt before automobile parts are plated or painted. This is called pickling the metal.

Hydrochlorides are also salts of hydrochloric acid. They are formed when the acid reacts with an organic base. Many drugs and medicines are hydrochlorides. *See also* ACID; BASE; CHLORIDE; HYDROCARBON.

D.M.H.W./A.D.

HYDROELECTRIC POWER (hī′ drō i lek′ trik paùr′) Hydroelectric power is power that is obtained from the energy of flowing water. If we want to, we could produce power from even little streams. Moving water can be made to turn wheels. The wheels can be made to turn electrical generators. The electricity would cost very little to produce. The country needs a vast electricity supply. So we usually harness the biggest rivers possible.

The most power comes from water that is falling a great distance. Water that is high up has high potential energy. We can tap this energy only when the water falls to a lower level. The name for the distance that the water falls is the head. The head of water in a slow-moving river may be only a few inches in many miles. This would not supply much power. The head of water in a waterfall may be thousands of times greater. Waterfalls are an excellent source of hydroelectric power. Unfortunately there are not enough natural waterfalls to meet our needs. We have to make our own.

By damming a stream or river, we can create artificial falls. The water builds up behind a dam, and the head increases. A dam built across a valley gives a head of water equal to the height of the dam. Hydroelectric schemes are often graded by their heads. A low scheme has a head under 31 m [100 ft]. A medium one has a head of 31 to 155 m [100 and 500 ft]. A high one is anything over 155 m [500 ft]. High schemes usually have sites up in mountainous areas. Here it is possible to dam whole valleys. Valuable land is not lost when the valley becomes flooded. Low-site schemes are usually at the outlets of rivers. They are sometimes called run-of-the-river schemes. The dam, or barrage, simply directs the river water so that if flows through turbines.

The powerhouse of a hydroelectric scheme is often built at the foot of the dam. Inside are the turbines. They have blades which are forced around by the water as it flows. The power of the turbines is used to work the electrical generators. There are several different kinds of turbines.

Different kinds of turbines are suitable for different heads of water. For medium and

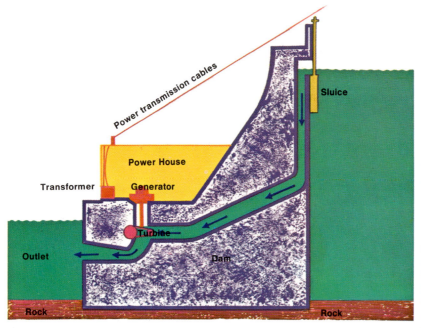

Left: diagram of a typical hydroelectric power station. When the sluice is lowered, the water behind the dam flows and turns the turbines, which turn the generators that make electricity. Transformers step up the electricty to very high voltage.

Below: three kinds of turbines used in hydroelectric systems. Pelton is an impulse type; Francis, a reaction type; Kaplan, a propeller type. Each is suited for different conditions.

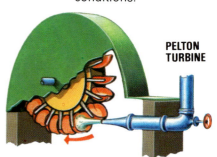

PELTON TURBINE

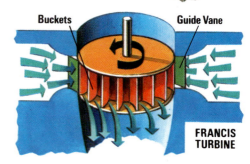

Buckets Guide Vane

FRANCIS TURBINE

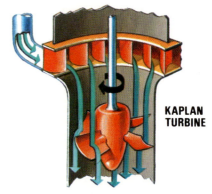

KAPLAN TURBINE

high heads, impulse turbines are often used. For medium and low heads, reaction turbines are used. The number and type of turbines depend upon how much power is to be generated. By turning the generators, the turbines produce electricity. Near to the powerhouse is a transformer. This is used to adjust the voltage of the supply fed into the grid. (*See* ELECTRICITY SUPPLY.)

The pipelines that carry water to the turbines are called penstocks. They lead from behind the dam through to the powerhouse. The powerhouse is sometimes located at a distance from the dam. The lower down it is, the greater the head will be. If the powerhouse is a long way away, another system is used. Water from the dam is led into a small reservoir called a forebay. It passes through a tunnel or an aqueduct. Penstocks carry the water from the forebay down to the powerhouse.

A surge shaft is another important part of a hydroelectric scheme. It is a safety device. When the flow of water to a turbine is cut down, there is a sudden build-up of pressure. This is due to the inertia of the water in the penstock. It could burst through and damage the turbine. The surge shaft is a way of absorbing the shock. It is a vertical pipe joining the bottom of the penstock to the outside. It opens above the highest level of the dam.

Some hydroelectric plants are able to store power. They have a pumped-storage system. When the demand for electricity is low, the turbines are not stopped. Instead the electricity is used to drive pumps. The pumps force water that has been through the turbines back up to the reservoir. This increases the head of water in the reservoir. It gives extra power when the demand for electricity is highest.

The world's biggest hydroelectric schemes are in the U.S.S.R. The largest is the plant at Krasnoyarsk. It is on the river Yenisey. It can produce 6,000 million watts (6,000 megawatts). In Canada, the plant at Churchill Falls can produce 5,225 megawatts.

Hydroelectric schemes have several advantages over other means of producing power. They do not use fuel. The turbines and other equipment are fairly simple and reliable. Once they are built, they need little maintenance. Few men are needed to run them. Many plants are run almost completely automatically. *See also* TIDAL POWER.

D.M.H.W./R.W.L.

HYDROFOIL (hī′ drə foil′) A hydrofoil is a structure on a motorboat which is designed to lift it out of the water as it gains speed. Trans-portation by water is usually much slower than transportation by land or air. A boat uses up most of its power overcoming the drag (resistance) of the water on its hull. For example, speedboats are designed so that they gradually lift out of the water as they increase speed. This reduces the area of hull in contact with the water, therefore reducing the drag. Heavier vessels cannot do this.

Hydrofoils are of such a shape that the flow of the water over them causes lift. (*See* AERODYNAMICS.) As the boat's speed increases, the hull lifts farther and farther out of the water until it is clear. The only parts then in contact with the water are the hydrofoils and supporting struts and the propeller shaft. Hydrofoils are of various designs. Some boats have V-shaped, or surface-piercing hydrofoils. Some have fully submerged foils. Others have variable-incidence (variable angle) foils that can be adjusted. In this way, the lift obtained is just enough to raise the hull of the boat out of the water.

Hydrofoil boats can travel very fast. They have the added advantage of making very little wash. One of the world's biggest hydrofoil boats is the U.S. Navy's AGEH-1. This boat has a service speed of 50 knots (91.7 kmph or 57 mph).

The power units in most hydrofoil boats are diesel engines. But many of the latest craft

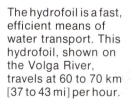

The hydrofoil is a fast, efficient means of water transport. This hydrofoil, shown on the Volga River, travels at 60 to 70 km [37 to 43 mi] per hour.

have gas turbine engines. Turbine engines are better suited to high-speed operation. Propulsion is generally by propellers which may be mounted on a separate shaft at the rear of the foils. For high-speed operation, specially designed propellers must be used. Propulsion may also be water-jet units driven by gas turbines and located at the base of the after foils, as in the Boeing PGH-2 Tucumcari naval patrol craft. Civil hydrofoils are in service in many countries, especially Scandinavia and the Soviet Union. J.J.A./R.W.L.

HYDROGEN (hī′ drə jən) Hydrogen is the first and simplest of all the elements. Its atomic number is 1, and it has the chemical symbol H. Hydrogen is a colorless, odorless, tasteless gas. Its atomic weight is 1.00797. At very low temperatures it becomes a solid. Solid hydrogen melts into a liquid at −259.2°C [−434.5°F]. At −252.8°C [−423°F], liquid hydrogen boils and becomes hydrogen gas. Hydrogen has a valence of 1 in all its compounds. (*See* VALENCE.)

Hydrogen is the most abundant element in

Hydrogen forms a large part of the stars, including this Trifid nebula in Sagittarius.

the universe. The sun and stars are made mostly of hydrogen. The gas is also spread very thinly throughout space. On earth, very little hydrogen gas is found. This is because the element is so reactive. It readily forms compounds with other elements. The most plentiful compound of hydrogen on earth is water. Each water molecule contains two hydrogen atoms linked to an oxygen atom. The formula for water is H_2O. Some hydrogen gas is found in natural gas. The gas is also found in the upper atmosphere.

All living things contain compounds of hydrogen. Hydrogen is found in carbohydrates, proteins, fats, and oils. Coal, petroleum, and natural gas all contain hydrogen compounds. They are mainly in the form of hydrocarbons. They were formed from the fossilized remains of plants that grew many millions of years ago. (*See* HYDROCARBON.)

Hydrogen gas can easily be made in the laboratory. Bubbles of the gas are formed when a metal such as zinc, sodium, or aluminum is added to dilute hydrochloric or sulfuric acid. Any metal above hydrogen in the electromotive series will replace hydrogen in the acids. (*See* ELECTROMOTIVE SERIES.)

Large amounts of hydrogen are produced for industry. The gas can be produced by treating natural gas, or gases from petroleum refining, with steam. The hydrocarbons are turned into hydrogen and carbon monoxide. Another method of production is the Bosch process. In this mixture of steam and carbon monoxide is passed over a catalyst. Hydrogen and carbon dioxide are formed. (*See* CATALYST.)

Very pure hydrogen can be produced by electrolysis. When an electric current is passed through water, the water splits up into the gases hydrogen and oxygen. Pure water will not conduct electricity. A little acid or alkali is added to it so that a current will pass.

Two-thirds of the hydrogen made in industry goes to make the gas ammonia. Ammonia is a compound of nitrogen and hydrogen. Its formula is NH_3. The process used to make ammonia is called the Haber process. (*See* HABER, FRITZ.) A large amount of hydrogen is also used to produce methanol. Different kinds of fuel can be made by treating coal, heavy oils, tar, and pitch with hydrogen. This process is called hydrogenation. It can also be used to change liquid vegetable oils into solid fats. This is known as the hardening of oils. Margarine is made in this way.

Hydrogen is extremely flammable. When it is mixed with oxygen, it forms an explosive mixture. The mixture is easily ignited. When hydrogen burns, great heat is produced. The gas is used in oxyhydrogen blowtorches to cut through and weld metal. Hydrogen can be used as a fuel. It makes a good fuel because burning it does not cause pollution. When hydrogen burns in air, only water is formed.

Hydrogen and oxygen are used in the rocket engines of spacecraft. They are also used to provide electricity and drinking water in these craft. They can be used in fuel cells. (*See* FUEL CELL.)

Hydrogen is the lightest element because its atoms are the simplest. The nucleus of a hydrogen atom is simply a proton, with a positive charge. In orbit around the nucleus is one electron, with a negative charge. If the electron is removed, the result is a hydrogen ion (H+). Acids contain hydrogen ions. (*See* ACID.)

Two hydrogen atoms come together to form a hydrogen molecule. They share their electrons between them. A hydrogen molecule is written H_2.

Hydrogen has two other isotopes. They are called deuterium and tritium. (*See* DEUTERIUM.) In deuterium, there is a neutron as well as a proton in the nucleus. A little deuterium is found mixed with ordinary hydrogen. If deuterium replaces the ordinary hydrogen in water, the result is heavy water. Its molecules are heavier than ordinary water because of the extra neutrons. Tritium contains three particles in its nucleus. There is

one proton and two neutrons. Tritium is an artificial isotope and is radioactive, but a minute amount occurs naturally. The normal form of hydrogen is sometimes called the protium isotope of hydrogen.

The sun and the stars produce vast amounts of energy from hydrogen. Atoms of hydrogen join together to form atoms of heavier elements. This is called fusion. During fusion, nuclear energy is released. For fusion to take place, the temperature must be very high. We rely on the fusion of hydrogen in the sun for the heat and light and all the energy that keeps us alive. *See also* FUSION.

D.M.H.W./J.R.W.

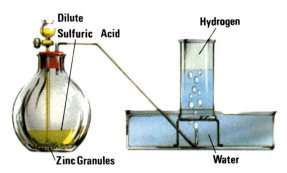

Apparatus for freeing hydrogen from sulphuric acid. Sulphuric acid reacts with zinc, releasing free hydrogen and forming zinc sulphate.

HYDROGEN BOND (hī′ drə jən bänd′) A hydrogen bond is a special chemical bond. It links hydrogen atoms inside molecules with other atoms. The other atoms may be in the same or in different molecules. Examples of hydrogen bonds are found between water molecules. Each water molecule contains two hydrogen atoms and one oxygen atom. The hydrogen atoms of each molecule have a positive electric charge. The oxygen atom has a negative electric charge. It attracts the positively charged electrons of the hydrogen atoms closer to it.

Opposite electric charges always attract each other. So the positively charged hydrogen atoms are attracted to the oxygen atoms of nearby water molecules. The water molecules cluster together in tight groups.

They are said to be joined by hydrogen bonds. This is the reason that water stays a liquid at ordinary temperatures. If the hydrogen bonds were not there the water molecules would separate. They drift away as water vapor. When water is heated, the water molecules move about more energetically. The hydrogen bonds are broken, and the water turns from liquid into vapor. Water molecules often link to other molecules by hydrogen bonds. They may form water of crystallization. (*See* HYDRATE.)

Hydrogen bonds are important in biochemistry. The twisted strands of the DNA molecule are held together by hydrogen bonds between the strands. (*See* NUCLEIC ACID.)

D.M.H.W./A.D.

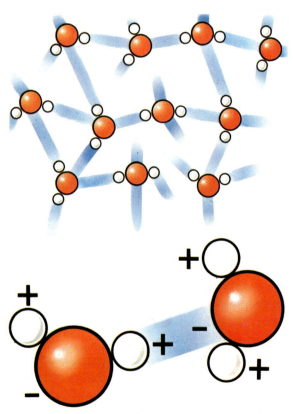

Hydrogen atoms have a positive electrical charge; oxygen atoms have a negative charge. These unlike charges attract each other.

HYDROGEN PEROXIDE (hī′ drə jən pə räk′ sīd′) Hydrogen peroxide is a colorless, syrupy liquid. Each molecule contains two atoms of hydrogen and two atoms of oxygen. It has the formula H_2O_2. Its boiling point is 152°C [305°F]. It solidifies at −2°C [28.4°F]. Hydrogen peroxide is unstable. Sunlight and heat make it break up into water and oxygen.

Because it yields oxygen so readily, hydrogen peroxide is a strong oxidizing agent. (*See* OXIDATION AND REDUCTION.) It may set fire to some substances. Pure hydrogen peroxide causes blisters on the skin. It is sometimes used as a rocket propellant.

For most uses, hydrogen peroxide is diluted with water. A 6% solution is called 20-volume peroxide because it can give up 20 times its own volume of oxygen gas. The solution is used as a bleach for hair and textiles, and as a disinfectant. A 3% solution (10-volume peroxide) is often used as a mouthwash.

Hydrogen peroxide is produced by the action of sulfuric acid on barium peroxide. It can also be produced by electrolysis of ammonium sulfate solution or concentrated sulfuric acid. (*See* ELECTROLYSIS.)

D.M.H.W./A.D.

HYDROGEN SULFIDE (hī′ drə jən səl′ fīd′) Hydrogen sulfide is a colorless, poisonous gas. It has the formula H_2S. It liquefies at −62°C [−79.6°F] and freezes at −82.9°C [−117.2°F].

The gas has a strong odor of rotten eggs. This is because eggs and other animal and vegetable matter contain sulfur compounds. Hydrogen sulfide gas is formed from these compounds as they decay. The gas is also found in nature in the mineral water from sulfur springs, in the gases from volcanoes, and in some oil wells. Hydrogen sulfide in the air turns coins and metal objects black. A layer of metal sulfide forms over them.

Hydrogen sulfide can be made by treating ferrous sulfide with hydrochloric or sulfuric acid. (*See* KIPPS APPARATUS.) In the laboratory, the gas can be used to identify and separate substances. If it is bubbled through a solution of a metal salt, it often causes the metal sulfide to form. This can be separated from other substances. (*See* CHEMICAL ANALYSIS.)   D.M.H.W./A.D.

HYDROLOGY (hīdräl′əjē) Hydrology is

the study of the surface and underground water found on the continents. Hydrologists are scientists who study water. They study what chemicals are found in water, the characteristics of water, and how water flows in rivers, pipes, and underground streams. By studying these things, the hydrologist can help engineers build canals, sewers, and roads that will not wash out during floods or heavy rains. The hydrologist also helps towns and cities to locate underground sources of water for domestic use. Hydrologists have learned a lot about floods. They have helped design and build many flood-control dams. By making a few measurements and using a formula, they can figure out how much water is held behind a dam and how much water is able to spill over the top. By studying the water cycle, hydrologists can learn where water comes from and where it goes. (*See* WATER CYCLE.) They also try to save water and prevent soil erosion. *See also* HYDRAULICS; HYDROELECTRIC POWER; WATER.   S.R.G./W.R.S.

Hydrologists study lake and river systems of the world. Of special interest to them is the Mississippi-Missouri system. Above: the Missouri River in Montana.

HYDROLYSIS(hī dräl′ ə səs)Hydrolysis is

a chemical reaction in which a substance is broken down by the action of water. During the reaction, the water itself divides into hydrogen ions (H+) and hydroxyl ions (OH−). The ions link up with different parts of the substance, and form new compounds.

Salts can be hydrolyzed. They form two new compounds. One is an acid, and the other is a base. Sodium carbonate, for example, forms carbonic acid and sodium hydroxide. Carbonic acid is only a weak acid, but sodium hydroxide is a strong base. The solution that forms will therefore be more basic, or alkaline. (*See* ALKALI; BASE.)

In organic chemistry, esters can be hydrolyzed to form organic acids and alcohols. Acids or bases may have to be added to make hydrolysis take place. When an ester is hydrolyzed by boiling with a base, it forms an alcohol and a salt of the organic acid. Soaps are made in this way. The process is called saponification.

Hydrolysis also occurs in the digestion of foods. Enzymes help to bring about the hydrolysis of food into simple compounds that our bodies can use. (*See* ENZYMES.)   D.M.H.W./A.D.

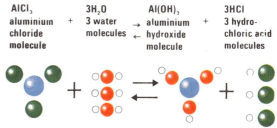

The hydrolysis of aluminum chloride into hydrochloric acid and aluminum hydroxide. As shown by the double arrows, the reaction is reversible.

HYDROMETER (hī dräm′ ət ər) A hy-

drometer is an instrument that is used to make measurements of the relative density of liquids. (*See* RELATIVE DENSITY.) It is a glass tube with a weight on one end and numbers printed on the side. When the tube is set in liquid, the bottom of it sinks into the liquid to a certain depth, depending upon the relative density of the liquid. The surface of the liquid reaches one of the numbers on the side. That number indicates the relative density of the liquid. If the tube sinks deeply, the liquid's surface reaches a number near the top of the tube, indicating a low relative density. If the tube sinks only a little, the liquid's surface reaches only the numbers at the bottom of the tube, indicating a high relative density. A hydrometer works on the principle that a floating body displaces its own weight in a liquid. (*See* ARCHIMEDES' PRINCIPLE.) Hydrometers are used in many different liquids to tell if they are pure.　　　　　　　　　S.R.G./R.W.L.

Hydrometers are used to measure the specific gravity of liquids. Different kinds of hydrometers are used for different kinds of liquids. Shown are: 1. a general purpose model; 2. a saccharometer for testing sugar solutions; 3. a general purpose model used for testing liquids that are heavier than water.

HYDROPONICS (hī′ drə pän′ iks) Hydroponics is the science of cultivating plants without soil. Instead of receiving nourish-ment from the soil, plants receive nourishment from water that has had nutrients (foods) added to it. Plants are grown in tanks containing gravel or coarse sand. The water is pumped through the gravel or sand periodically. Some plants are grown in tanks that contain only water. Hydroponics is also called soilless agriculture, nutriculture, and chemical culture. The science was developed in the 1800s, but it has never been used on a large scale by commercial growers.

Plants grown by this method must receive the same amount of light and warmth they would get if they were growing in soil. Growers who use hydroponic methods indoors must provide artificial light and heat.

There are two main methods of growing plants without soil, water culture and gravel culture.

Water culture is a method in which the plants are suspended with their roots in a tank of water. Nutrients like potassium nitrate, ammonium and aluminum sulfates, and calcium sulfate are added to the water. Manganous sulfate and ferrous sulfate are also added. Air is regularly pumped into the solution to replace air used up by the roots.

Gravel culture is a less complicated method of growing plants without soil. The plant roots are placed in coarse sand or gravel, and a nutrient solution is pumped through the material. In a variation of the gravel culture, the nutrient solution slowly drips from tiny tubes beside each plant. In this way, each plant can be fed more directly.

Scientists have not yet been able to prove that hydroponics produces better and larger crops. Some scientists have suggested that hydroponics would be ideal for growing crops in places were soil does not exist, like on ships at sea, frozen Arctic areas, and orbiting space stations.　　　　　　　W.R.P./F.W.S.

HYDROSTATICS (hī′ drə stat′ iks) Hydrostatics is one of the branches of physics that deal with the properties and behavior of

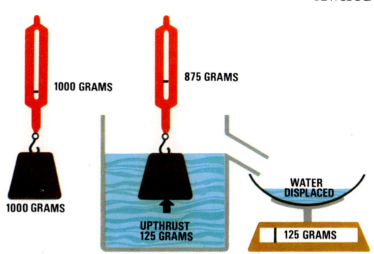

The first law of hydrostatics—Archimedes' principle—states that a floating or submerged object experiences an upthrust equal to the weight of the water it displaces. Right: a weight is hung from a scale. When immersed in water, the weight appears to weigh less. The weight of the water displaced equals the loss in weight.

liquids. It deals with liquids that are stationary. For example, it deals with water in a glass tank, the way the water presses against the sides, and the way anything floating in the tank behaves. The study of fluids that are moving is called hydrokinetics. Hydrostatics and hydrokinetics are linked together in the study of hydrodynamics.

In hydrostatics, there are three important principles, or laws that were discovered many years ago.

The first law   The first law of hydrostatics deals with objects that are floating or immersed in liquids. It is also called Archimedes' principle. Archimedes was an ancient Greek scientist who discovered the principle over 2,200 years ago. The law states that a body floating or submerged in a liquid loses as much weight as the weight of the liquid that it displaces (pushes out of the way).

It is easy for us to tell that we lose weight when we are in water. It is also easy to see that we displace water. If a person climbs into an absolutely full bath, then a lot of water will spill over.

The principle is important in ships. When a ship has no cargo, it floats high in the water. It displaces only a little water. When it is heavily laden with cargo, it sinks much lower in the water. It displaces a greater amount of water. If the weight of the ship and the cargo

becomes greater than the weight of water the ship can displace, then the ship will sink.

The second law   The second law of hydrostatics was stated in 1586 by the Dutch mathematician Simon Stevin. This law says that the pressure on a given point of a submerged body is equal to the weight of fluid directly above that point. A fluid may be a gas, or a mixture of gases, such as the atmosphere. This means that at the surface of the earth, the weight of several miles of atmosphere is pressing down upon us. High in the mountains, or higher still in airplanes, the pressure of the atmosphere is reduced.

At the deepest points in the ocean, the pressure is extremely great. Here there is the pressure of hundreds of meters of salt water as well as the atmospheric pressure on top of that. The pressure may be several tons per square centimeter.

The third law   The third law of hydrostatics is also called Pascal's theorem. It was named for the French scientist Blaise Pascal. He discovered it in 1648. The law states that pressures applied to a contained liquid are transmitted equally throughout the liquid, in every direction.

The last two laws of hydrostatics are very important in engineering. Marine engineers, for example, must work out how strong to make the hulls of submarines to withstand underwater pressures. Dam-builders must be able to calculate how thick to build their dams. The laws are specially important in hydraulics. *See also* HYDRAULICS.

D.M.H.W./R.W.L.

HYDROXIDE (hī dräk′ sīd) A hydroxide is a chemical compound that contains a hydroxyl (−OH) group. Hydroxides can be thought of as compounds formed from water. One of the hydrogen atoms in H_2O has been changed for another atom, or group of atoms. In organic chemistry, there are many compounds with OH groups. However, these are usually called hydroxy compounds, not hydroxides.

Many, but not all hydroxides are bases. (*See* BASES.) Solutions of sodium and potassium hydroxides are very strong bases. The molecules split up in the water to give hydroxyl ions (OH−). Bases that dissolve in water are called alkalis. The most important alkali is sodium hydroxide. Other names for it are caustic soda and soda lye. Another important alkali is potassium hydroxide, or caustic potash.

A solution of calcium hydroxide is called limewater. It is used to detect carbon dioxide gas. When carbon dioxide is bubbled through it, the solution becomes milky. This is because white particles of calcium carbonate are formed.

The hydroxides of certain metals may be produced by adding soluble hydroxides, such as sodium hydroxide, to soluble salts of the metal. For example, zinc hydroxide may be made by adding sodium hydroxide to zinc sulfate solution.

Soluble hydroxides may be made by electrolyzing solutions of salts. (*See* ELECTROLYSIS.) Sodium hydroxide forms during the electrolysis of sodium chloride (common salt) solution.

D.M.H.W./A.D.

HYENA (hī ē′ nə) Hyenas are doglike nocturnal carnivores that belong to the family Hyaenidae. Hyenas feed on the remains of dead animals. They also hunt animals for food. Hyenas have strong jaws and teeth, enabling them to crush and eat even large bones.

The spotted hyena (*Crocuta crocuta*) lives in Africa. Its fur is yellowish gray with black spots. It is known for its strange howl that sounds like a hysterical human laugh. The striped hyena (*Hyaena hyaena*) lives in northern Africa and parts of Asia. Smaller than the spotted hyena, the striped hyena has a grayish coat. Narrow black stripes run across its body and legs. The brown hyena (*Hyaena brunnea*) lives mainly in southern Africa. It has long hair on its back and stripes only on its legs. Frequently poisoned and shot by farmers, the brown hyenas are now endangered. *See also* AARDWOLF.

J.J.A./J.J.M.

HYGIENE (hī′ jēn′) Hygiene is the branch of science and medicine that has to do with maintaining a healthy body and mind. If a body is generally fit and healthy, it is much more able to withstand disease or to recover quickly from an illness or accident.

To keep healthy, the body has many needs. Among the most important are fresh air, light, warmth, cleanliness, and a balanced diet. The diet should consist of the right kinds of food and drink. Supplies of food and water must be fresh and clean, and therefore

Electrolysis plant for producing sodium hydroxide.

not contaminated with vermin. Regular washing, proper sanitation, proper sleep, and regular exercise all aid in personal health.

Although a person can do much to guard his health, some threats to health can be prevented by the action of communities. For example, governments enforce laws to control pollution of the air and water. Laws are also passed to protect workers in factories or other places from various hazards. Clean water supplies and the disposal of garbage and sewage are usually the responsibility of public utilities or authorities. Governmental bodies, such as the United States Food and Drug Administration, make sure hygienic standards are kept in food processing industries. (*See* FOOD PRESERVATION.) At the international level, the World Health Organization develops national programs to fight disease and prevent its spread. *See also* MEDICINE; MENTAL HEALTH; NUTRITION; SEWAGE TREATMENT. J.J.A./J.J.F.

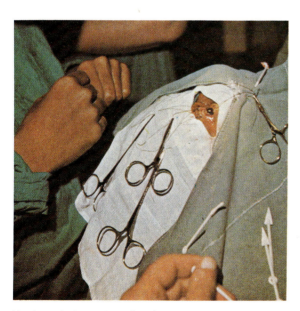

Hygiene is important for the eye operation above.

HYGROMETER (hī gräm′ ət ər) A hygrometer is an instrument that measures the water vapor content of the air. It is used by meteorologists to determine relative humidity. There are two main types of hygrometers: the psychrometer and the hair hygrometer.

A psychrometer consists of two thermometers. One thermometer gives the actual temperature. The bulb of the other thermometer is wrapped in muslin and kept moist with water. In order to determine the humidity, the psychrometer is spun at about 14 km [9 mi] per hour. Water evaporates from the wet-bulb thermometer, thus lowering its temperature reading. (*See* EVAPORATION.) If the humidity is high, less water will evaporate.

The wet-bulb thermometer reading is always less than the dry-bulb reading, unless there is 100% relative humidity. The difference between the thermometer readings is called the wet-bulb depression. Using this information, the relative humidity can be determined by referring to special tables.

A hair hygrometer uses human hair to determine the humidity. The hair absorbs moisture from the air, becoming longer if the humidity is high. A lever moves according to the change in hair length, indicating the relative humidity. J.M.C./C.R.

HYPHA (hī′ fə) Hyphae are the threadlike parts of a fungus that make up the mycelium. A hypha can consist of one or more cells. It may branch out and join with another hypha to form a dikaryon, which may eventually permit sexual reproduction. On the other hand, the tip of a hypha may separate to form spores called conidia. These break off, germinate, and grow into new fungi by asexual reproduction. *See also* MOLD. W.R.P./E.R.L.

HYPNOSIS (hip nō′ səs) Hypnosis is a state in which the mind becomes less aware of the surrounding world. The subject (person under hypnosis) may seem to be asleep, but can still respond to outside events. Easily influenced by suggestion, the subject can control many body functions that are normally automatic. For example, a hypnotized person may be insensitive to pain if he or she is told that he feels nothing.

A person is generally put into a state of hypnosis by another person, called a hypnotist. But hypnosis can also be brought about by the subject himself. This is called self-hypnosis or autohypnosis.

If performed by a hypnotist, the hypnotist talks to the subject slowly, repeating his words over and over again. Eventually the subject is completely relaxed, and goes into a trance (a hypnotic state).

Not everyone can be hypnotized. People cannot be hypnotized against their wills. Subjects do not do anything under hypnosis that is against their ideas or principles. But hypnosis is not a game. It can be extremely dangerous when performed by an untrained person.

Hypnosis is often used in place of an anesthetic during surgery or childbirth. The patient feels nothing but can cooperate with the surgeon. Hallucinations can also be induced under hypnosis. A hypnotized person may be able to recall forgotten events in his early life. This ability has been used by psychiatrists to treat certain mental illnesses. *See also* PSYCHIATRY; PSYCHOANALYSIS. J.J.A./J.J.F.

HYSTERESIS (his′ tə rē′ səs) Hysteresis is a lag that occurs when an attempt is made to alter the magnetism of an object. To make a piece of iron magnetic, the iron can be placed in a strong magnetic field. (*See* FIELD; MAGNETISM.) As the strength of the field is increased, the magnetism of the iron grows. Eventually it cannot become any more magnetic. It is said to be saturated with magnetism. If the magnetic field is taken away, some of the magnetism in the iron remains.

To remove the magnetism from the iron, an opposite magnetic field must be applied. This field will have to reach a certain strength before the iron becomes nonmagnetic. If the strength of the field is increased as before, the iron will again become magnetic. Its magnetism will be in the opposite direction. Eventually it will again become saturated. However, there is always a lag between the change

in strength of the magnetic field and the change in magnetism of the iron. It is the resistance to change in magnetism that forms hysteresis.

The hysteresis that occurs with different substances can be measured. A hysteresis loop is drawn to show what happens as an object is gradually magnetized and then demagnetized. Soft iron is much easier to demagnetize than hard steel. The best permanent magnets are made of materials that are very difficult to demagnetize. They are made of specially produced alloys that provide wide hysteresis loops.

The hysteresis motor is a kind of electric motor that relies on hysteresis to keep a constant speed. A constant speed is needed specially in electric clocks and record players.

Hysteresis occurs in many systems. It is very important in elasticity, or the stretching properties of elastic bodies. D.M.H.W./J.T.

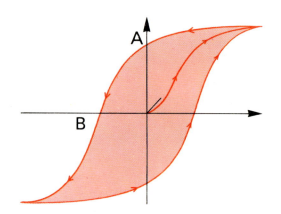

Plotting a graph of magnetometer deflection against increasing electric current put through an electromagnet gave this hysteresis loop. The magnetometer is deflected at A when when the core is magnetized. To demagnetize the core, the current must be reversed and increased to reach B.

IBIS (ī′ bəs) Ibises are tall birds that belong to the family Threskiornithidae. They are closely related to the herons. (*See* HERON.) Ibises have long necks, bills, and legs. They wade in shallow water and catch small fish, reptiles, and amphibians. There are four species of ibis in North America. Three species are found only in the southeastern part of the United States and parts of Mexico. The fourth species, the white-faced ibis, is found in west-central United States and Mexico. *See also* SPOONBILL.   S.R.G./M.L.

The scarlet ibis lives in tropical South America.

ICE (īs) Ice is the solid form of water. When water is cooled, it contracts (shrinks) until its temperature drops to 4°C [39°F]. It then expands until the temperature drops to 0°C [32°F], the freezing point of water. It remains ice until the temperature goes above the freezing point. It then melts, although the temperature of the water remains at 0°C [32°F] until all the ice has melted.

Ice has a greater volume than water, but its density is slightly less. This is why ice floats in a glass of water.

When ice freezes, hydrogen bonds form a rigid structure of six-sided crystals. The type of crystal structure depends on how the water is frozen. Forms of ice include snow, sleet, frost, and hail.   J.M.C./C.R.

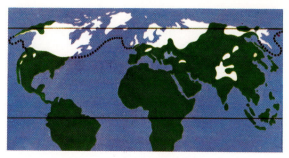

The maximal extent of glacial ice in the Ice Age.

ICE AGE (īs āj) An ice age was a period of the earth's history when large areas of the globe were covered by glaciers and ice sheets. The most recent ice age occurred during the Pleistocene epoch, which ended about 10,000 years ago. There is also evidence that other ice ages have occurred. An ice age took place during Precambrian times, about 700 million years ago. Another ice age occurred during the late Carboniferous and early Permian periods, about 280 million years ago.

The Pleistocene ice age   The last ice age began about 600,000 years ago during the Pleistocene epoch. The ice advanced southward during four periods called glacial ages. These glacial ages are separated by interglacial ages, when the ice retreated. The glacial ages, from oldest to most recent, are called the Nebraskan, the Kansan, the Illinoian, and the Wisconsin. The interglacial ages are called the Aftonian, the Yarmouth, and the Sangamon. A typical glacial age lasts about 40,000 to 60,000 years. Interglacial ages last about 40,000 years. Geologists have suggested that the earth may now be in an interglacial age.

Scientists have learned a great deal about the ice ages by studying fossils and other evidence from the Pleistocene epoch. Geologists believe that great ice sheets were centered near Hudson Bay in North America and on the Scandinavian peninsula in Europe. The ice became thick, and flowed out from these centers. All of Canada and the northern third of the United States, as far south as New York City and the Missouri River valley, were covered by ice. In places, the ice was 2,400 to 3,000 m [8,000 to 10,000 ft] thick. In Europe, ice covered all of northern Europe, the British Isles, and much of northern Russia. At times during the Pleistocene epoch, more than 30% of the earth's surface was covered with ice.

The Pleistocene glaciations had a profound effect on the landscape of not only those areas affected by the ice cover but those directly south. Because the climatic zones were shifted southward, plants and animals were forced to live in more restricted environments. Fjords, moraines, and drumlins were created by the retreating ice. Many lakes, including the Great Lakes, were formed during the last ice age.

There is no accepted explanation of the cause of ice ages. Some geologists believe that the continents were in different positions at the start of the ice ages, but have since moved. (*See* CONTINENTAL DRIFT.) Other scientists believe that the sun's light and warmth may have been blocked, perhaps by volcanic ash in the atmosphere. (*See* VOLCANO.) In recent years, some geologists have theorized that the Antarctic ice sheet fluctuates in size. When the ice sheet expands, it causes a drop in the earth's temperature. This temperature drop may spark the beginning of an ice age.   J.M.C./W.R.S.

ICEBERG (īs′ bərg′) An iceberg is a large, floating mass of ice. Icebergs break away, or calve, from the glaciers and ice sheets along the coasts of Greenland and Antarctica. They sometimes present a major hazard to shipping.

A glacier often extends slightly into the sea. Eventually, cracks form in the ice, and a piece of the glacier breaks off, perhaps during stormy weather. Greenland is the source of most North Atlantic icebergs. These icebergs may be taller than 90 m [300 ft]. Antarctic icebergs are often very large, but are usually flat-topped. One huge Antarctic iceberg had an area of 31,000 sq km [12,000 sq mi].

Usually, only one-ninth of an iceberg is visible above water. As an iceberg floats, some of the ice melts and pieces break off. Eventually, it completely disappears.

In 1912, the British ocean liner Titanic hit an iceberg and sank in the North Atlantic. More than 1,500 people died. Since then, the United States and other countries have formed an International Ice Patrol. The patrol, operated by the United States Coast Guard, uses ships, planes, and radar to locate icebergs. *See also* GLACIATION.   J.M.C./W.R.S.

ICELAND SPAR (ī′ slənd spär′) Iceland spar is a transparent variety of calcite. It is so called because Iceland is the chief source of this mineral. Iceland spar has the property of double refraction. This means that if a piece of this mineral is placed over a line of type in a book, for instance, a person sees "double." Instead of one line of type, he sees two. The property of double refraction makes it possible to use Iceland spar to produce polarized light. Many optical instruments have polarizers made of Iceland spar. (*See* POLARIZED LIGHT.)   J.J.A./R.H.

ICHEUMON FLY (ik nü′ mən flī) Ichneumon flies are insects belonging to the same group as bees and wasps (order Hymenoptera). Ichneumon flies are not true flies. They have four membranous wings. Flies have only two. Some types of this insect are about the size of a small ant. Others grow to 6 cm [2.3 in] in length, including the ovipositor. They do not sting people.

The female's body ends in a pointed egg-laying tool called an ovipositor. The ovipositor may be up to twice the length of the body. The three threadlike parts of this organ form a tube. With it, the insect places eggs in the bodies of caterpillars or other larvae and pupae. The parasitic larvae remain where they are placed until full grown. The larvae often kill the insect on which they live as parasites.

Ichneumon flies are important to farmers. The insects often feed on other insects that destroy plants. The ichneumon fly larvae eats insects in the egg, larval, and pupal stages. Ichneumon flies destroy caterpillars especially. These insects also attack spiders and the larvae of certain beetles, flies, and wasps.

J.J.A./J.E.R.

An ichneumon fly, a relative of bees and wasps.

ICHTHYOLOGY (ik′ thē äl′ ə jē) The study of fishes is called ichthyology. It includes the study of the bodies of fishes, the evolution of fishes, how and where the fishes live, and their relationships to other fishes and animals. Ichthyologists, people who study fishes, do many different things. Some ichthyologists study only the fish itself. They cut open the body and learn how it is put together. Other ichthyologists travel all over the world studying where the thousands of different kinds of fishes live. Besides learning about the fishes, the scientists learn a lot about how the earth used to be. Still other ichthyologists study the number of fishes that live in certain places. They start programs to help increase the numbers of fishes. They also help fishermen so that they may catch more fish. Many scientists decide how many fish can be caught without hurting the whole population of fishes. *See also* CONSERVATION.

S.R.G./E.C.M.

ICHTHYOSAUR (ik′ thē ə sȯr′) An ichthyosaur was a fishlike reptile that lived in the Mesozoic era. (*See* MESOZOIC ERA.) It became extinct at the end of that era. There have been many fossils of ichthyosaurs found. They resembled the sharks of today, except they had a long beaklike mouth with many sharp teeth. *See also* FISH; FOSSIL; REPTILE; SHARK.

S.R.G./E.C.M.

ICONOSCOPE (ī kän′ ə skōp′) Iconoscope is the name given to the cathode-ray tube that first made television transmission possible. The iconoscope was invented in the early 1900s by Vladimir K. Zworykin, a Russian physicist. The iconoscope is shaped like a light bulb. It has a thin neck, but it is usually much larger than a light bulb.

Light enters the lens of the television camera, and is focused on a photoelectric surface inside the tube. The photoelectric surface changes the light rays into electrical impulses. The photoelectric surface is made up of tiny, light-sensitive beads spread on a sheet of mica. An electron gun is enclosed in the neck of the tube. The gun sprays a stream of electrons across the photoelectric surface. The amount of light that falls on the surface causes the amount of positive electric charge on the surface to vary. And the beams of light

Iconoscope (above) was a type of cathode ray tube used in early television cameras.

coming through the television lens are changed to electric charges. These charges become the electric waves that make up the broadcast.

The image orthicon has replaced the iconoscope in today's television broadcasting. It is much smaller, and more sensitive to light. Thus, it allows television cameras to operate in conditions where the lighting is dim.　　　　　　　　　　　　W.R.P./J.T.

IDEAL MECHANICAL ADVANTAGE A
certain force is needed to lift an object. A machine allows you to use less force than if you lifted it on your own. Some machines, such as a pulley, can be used to lift objects. The ratio of the weight lifted to the force needed is called the mechanical advantage (mi kan′ i kəl əd vant′ ij) of the machine. The mechanical advantage is always greater than one. For a simple machine, the mechanical advantage can be calculated. The calculated mechanical advantage is called the ideal mechanical advantage. In practice, the mechanical advantage is always less than the ideal mechanical advantage. This means that, in practice, a slightly greater force is needed to lift an object. This difference is due mainly to friction. (*See* FRICTION.)　　M.E./J.T.

IGNEOUS ROCK (ig′ nē əs räk′) Igneous
rock forms from the cooling and crystallization of a hot, molten material called magma. Magma is molten rock that has been subjected to great temperature and pressure beneath the earth's surface. There are two main types of igneous rock: extrusive and intrusive.

Extrusive rock is magma forced from the earth's interior through a volcano or a crack in the earth's surface. This magma, called lava when it reaches the earth's surface, quickly cools when it is exposed to air. Because of the rapid cooling, extrusive rock contains small crystals and is fine-textured. Extrusive igneous rocks include basalt, obsidian, and pumice.

Intrusive rock forms when magma cools below the surface and in pre-existing rock forms. The magma sometimes cools in large masses called batholiths. It may also cool in vertical bands called dikes or in horizontal layerlike bands called sills. Because intrusive rock cools and hardens slowly, it contains large crystals and is coarse-textured. Granite is an intrusive igneous rock.

Igneous rocks contain a variety of minerals, including quartz, mica, and feldspar.
　　　　　　　　　　　　J.M.C./W.R.S.

Some of the earth's oldest and most recent rocks are igneous. Shown here is the lava shore of the island of Surtsey, formed by a volcano in 1963.

IGUANA (ig wän′ ə) An iguana is a large
lizard that belongs to the family Iguanidae. There are many different species of iguanas in the world. Most of them live in South America and on islands in the Pacific Ocean. The best-known species of iguana is one living on the Galapagos Islands. It may reach a

length of 1.5 m [5 ft]. Named the marine iguana, it is the only marine lizard in the world. *See also* LIZARD; REPTILE.

S.R.G./R.L.L.

ILLUMINATION (il ü′ mə nā′ shən) Illumination is the creation of artificial light. The earliest means of illumination were open fires and burning torches. Candles, kerosene lamps and lanterns, and gas lamps were developed later. Incandescent electric lights were introduced in 1879 by Thomas Edison. Today, most of our illumination is accomplished with incandescent lights. (*See* INCANDESCENCE.)

The neon light, developed in 1911 by French physicist Georges Claude, is used largely to illuminate commercial signs and displays. The fluorescent lamp is one of the most recent developments in illumination. It produces a brighter light than an incandescent light bulb. Fluorescent bulbs are long, narrow tubes. They are used mostly to light office buildings and other commercial and public structures. (*See* FLUORESCENCE.) Sodium and mercury vapor lamps are used to illuminate highways and other outdoor public areas.

In photometry, illumination is the luminous flux incident per unit area expressed in lumens per unit of area. (*See* PHOTOMETRY.) *See also* ELECTRIC LIGHT. W.R.P./J.T.

IMAGINARY NUMBER (im aj′ ə nər′ ē nəm′ bər) If a number is multiplied by itself, the result is another number. This number is the square of the first number. The first number is the square root of the second number. If the square root is positive, then so is the square. If the square root is negative, then the square is still positive. This is because a negative times a negative gives a positive. This means that both positive and negative numbers give a positive number when squared. What, then, is the square root of a negative number? A special number has to be used. Its symbol is i and it is the square root of minus one, $\sqrt{-1}$. Suppose you want to know the square root of -16. The square root of $+16$ is 4 (or -4). Therefore, the square root of -16 can be written as 4i. The square of 4i is $4 \times i \times 4 \times i$. This equals $4 \times 4 \times i \times i$. 4×4 is 16 and $i \times i$ is $\sqrt{-1} \times \sqrt{-1}$ which is -1. Therefore, the square of 4i is -1×16 which equals -16. Numbers such as i and 4i are called imaginary numbers. M.E./S.P.A.

IMMISCIBLE LIQUID (im is′ ə bəl lik′ wəd) Two liquids are immiscible if they cannot be mixed together. A common example is oil and water. If you try to mix them together, a boundary forms between the two. The lighter liquid, usually the oil, lies above the heavier liquid. Certain liquids, such as ethyl alcohol and water, can be mixed together. They are said to be miscible. Whether two

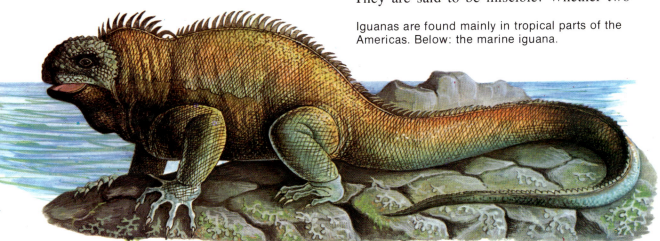

Iguanas are found mainly in tropical parts of the Americas. Below: the marine iguana.

liquids mix or not depends on their chemical properties. If they resemble each other chemically, they are usually miscible. For example, the molecules of both water and alcohol have an −OH group. Because of this, they are miscible. On the other hand, water and oil are very different chemically and so are immiscible. M.E./A.D.

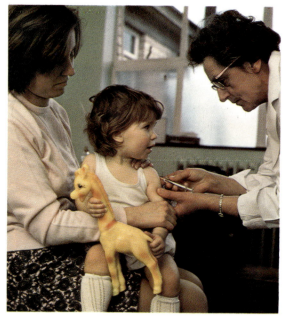

A child is being vaccinated. In this way, immunity to many diseases can be given.

IMMUNITY (im yü′ nət ē) Immunity is the ability of the body to resist certain harmful substances that enter it. The substances include disease-producing organisms such as bacteria and viruses. The body has natural immunity to many bacteria and viruses that cause disease in other creatures. Other diseases attack the body. The body's defenses work to overcome them. In this way, the body can gain immunity. If it builds up a permanent defense, disease cannot attack that body again for a long period. In some cases, the immunity lasts for the rest of a person's life.

Through immunization, a person can be given immunity to many diseases without first catching the disease. Immunization is any medical procedure that makes a person able to develop immunity to specific disease-producing organisms. (See VACCINATION.)

The job of fighting invading germs, such as bacteria, is chiefly carried out by the lymphatic system and the lymphocytes. The lymphocytes are a type of white blood cell produced in lymphatic tissue. The action of these cells depends on their recognition of the invading germs as ''foreign.'' By some method that is not properly understood, the lymphocytes react to the presence of any protein that does not belong to the body itself. This includes the proteins that make up germs. This reaction is called an immune reaction.

The lymphocytes then deal with the foreign protein in various ways. They may produce antitoxins. Antitoxins are chemical substances that neutralize (make harmless) the toxins (poisons) produced by the germs. The lymphocytes may also produce antibodies. Antibodies cause the disease-producing bacteria to agglutinate (stick together in clumps). Both antitoxins and antibodies are highly specific. In other words, they can fight only a particular type of disease-producing germ, or a few types that are very closely related. This is why catching chicken pox does not give immunity to smallpox. However, catching cowpox does give immunity to smallpox. The viruses that cause cowpox and smallpox are very similar.

The production of antitoxins and antibodies is too slow to stop invading germs that cause disease the first time they enter the body. But they may continue to circulate in the blood, ready to react immediately if infection occurs again. In other cases, the body may be able to make the antitoxin or antibody much more quickly a second time. This is why the common diseases of childhood, such as mumps, chicken pox, and measles, usually strike only once. Such acquired immunity is called active immunity. The body has actively produced its own antibodies. Immunity can also be passive. In this way, the body can acquire ready-made antibodies. A baby acquires immunity to many diseases in this way. It absorbs antibodies from its mother's bloodstream before birth and from her milk afterwards. Such protection, however, is short-lived.

Artificial immunity through vaccination may also be active or passive. Active immunity can be acquired by injecting dead germs into the body, or injecting a type of the living germ that causes only a slight discomfort. In some cases, a toxoid is used. A toxoid is a bacterial poison that has been made harmless. Each of these methods may stimulate the body to make antibodies or antitoxins.

Passive immunity is given by injecting a serum. (*See* INJECTION.) This is obtained from the blood of an infected person or animal that has produced the right antibodies.

In the case of most diseases caused by viruses, vaccination remains medicine's basic weapon. Diseases caused by viruses range from a common cold to smallpox and polio. These viruses are unaffected by antibiotics and the sulfa drugs. But in 1957 it was discovered that the body has a second type of immune response to viruses apart from that involving antibodies. It was found that body cells attacked by viruses make a substance called interferon. Interferon passes to neighboring cells, helping them to resist the spread of the viruses. It has been found that interferon from a particular species protects any creature of the same species from most types of viruses. But it does not protect any other species. Therefore human patients can only be protected with human interferon. This would be effective against a wide range of virus diseases.

The body's immune response to foreign protein is not always a help to medicine. The same mechanism is responsible for rejecting tissue transplanted from another person's body into a patient. (*See* TRANSPLANTATION.) The lymphocytes attack a transplanted heart or kidney in the same way as they attack invading bacteria.

The immune response can also be the cause of disease. Most scientists believe that a newborn child does not have the ability to reject foreign tissues. Its body learns this in the first year or two of life. At the same time, it learns not to attack its own tissues. If the body's ability to recognize its own tissues is somehow disrupted, an autoimmune disease may result. An autoimmune disease is a form of disease caused when the body's defense mechanism against infection begins to attack the body's own tissues. In quite another way, if the body becomes oversensitive to foreign proteins, the result may be an allergy, such as asthma or hay fever.   J.J.A./J.J.F.

IMPACT (im′ pakt′) Impact, in mechanics, is the striking of one body against another. In an automobile crash, impact happens at the moment of collision between the auto and another object. A law involving impact states that the total momentum (velocity times mass) of the bodies is the same before and after impact if both objects are elastic, and not effected by other forces.

In actual practice, some of the energy of momentum is absorbed while causing a permanent change in one, or both, of the bodies. The denting that occurs when two autos collide is an example of this. Since the mass of both bodies remains the same, the impact must result in a loss of velocity. The ratio between the differences of the velocities of the two bodies after impact to the same differences before impact is called the impact coefficient.   W.R.P./J.T.

IMPALA (im pal′ ə) The impala (*Aepyceros melampus*) is an African antelope known for its tremendous jumping ability. High jumps of more than 3 m [10 ft] and long jumps of 9 m [30 ft] have been recorded. Impalas are also swift runners. They may run as fast as 80 km [50 mi] per hour.

Standing from 84 to 94 cm [33 to 37 in] at the shoulder, impalas weigh from 45 to 82 kg

These impalas live in the bush country of southern and eastern Africa.

[100 to 180 lbs]. The animals have glossy, reddish brown coats on the top and sides. The tail and underparts are white. The male has a pair of slender horns up to 91 cm [3 ft] in length. The strongest males lead harem herds. These herds are made up of females and young. The other males live alone or stay together in bachelor herds.

Impalas live in many areas of East and South Africa. They rarely venture far from water. Impalas prefer bush country, where there is plenty of shelter. Their natural enemies include leopards, lions, and wild African hunting dogs. The impalas feed mainly on grass, leaves, and fruit.   J.J.A./J.J.M.

IMPEDANCE (im pēd' əns) Suppose that a battery is connected to an electric cicuit. The battery causes a potential difference to be set up between the two ends of the circuit. (*See* POTENTIAL.) This produces a current in the circuit. The size of the current depends on the size of the potential difference. It also depends on the components and the wire in the circuit. They always oppose the flow of current. If the current is a direct current, then it flows in one direction only. (*See* DIRECT CURRENT.) The opposition of a component or a wire is then called its resistance. (*See* RESISTANCE, ELECTRICAL.) If the current is an alternating current, its direction reverses at short intervals. (*See* ALTERNATING CURRENT.) The opposition to the flow is slightly different in this case and so it has a different name. It is called the impedance.

M.E./L.L.R.

IMPLANTATION (im' plan' tā' shən) Implantation is the process in most mammals by which a fertilized egg, or zygote, attaches itself to the uterine wall. (*See* UTERUS.) The wall of the uterus prepares for the arrival of the fertilized egg by becoming thickened with blood, water, and nutrients. (*See* MENSTRUAL CYCLE.) These changes take place because of the action of the female sex hormone progesterone.

When the fertilized egg touches the uterine wall, the egg burrows into the thickened tissue. The zygote stays embedded in the wall until birth. During this time, the embryo relies on the uterine lining for the environment it needs in which to grow and develop properly.

The term implantation is also used to describe the surgical insertion of a mechanical device or an artificial organ into the body of a living organism. (*See* TRANSPLANTATION.) *See also* GESTATION PERIOD; PREGNANCY; REPRODUCTIVE SYSTEM; SEX.   A.J.C./J.J.F.

IMPLOSION (im plō′ zhən) Implosion is the reverse of explosion. (*See* EXPLOSIVE.) An implosion occurs when a vessel collapses inward. This is caused by a difference in the air pressures outside and inside the vessel. Normally, the atmosphere pushes against both the inside and outside walls of an open flask with equal pressure. If, however, the neck of the flask is connected to a pump, and the air inside is gradually taken out, the internal pressure will decrease. Eventually, the pressure outside would be so great compared to the pressure inside that the flask would collapse inward, or implode.

A cathode-ray tube used in electronics contains a partial vacuum. When the tube is cracked, it usually implodes with great violence. The cracking weakens the wall of the tube, and the external pressure causes it to burst inward toward the lower pressure.   W.R.P./J.T.

INCAN CIVILIZATION (ing′ kən siv′ ə lə zā′ shən) The Incan civilization flourished in South America many years before the arrival of European explorers. The Inca Empire extended 4,020 km [2,500 mi] along the Pacific Ocean. Cuzco, the Inca capitol, was located in the Andes mountains.

The Incas had a highly organized government that directed the everyday lives of the citizens. Their main occupation was farming. The Incas were the first people to raise potatoes. They farmed the steep hillsides of the Andes, growing crops like squash, maize, beans, peanuts, cotton, and tomatoes.

The Incas domesticated the llama, using it for its wool and as a beast of burden. They ate llama and guinea pig meat, as well as the many vegetables they grew.

The Incas invented a calendar of considerable accuracy. Their year started on December 21, the summer solstice in the southern hemisphere. Their year was divided into 12 months of 30 days each. Each month was divided into three weeks of ten days each.

The Incas were great builders. They built a superb network of roads throughout the empire. Messengers relayed news by running between stations located at intervals along the roads. Rope suspension bridges hung over deep chasms.

Incas built magnificent temples and palaces out of stone. They also built irrigation canals to maintain an adequate water supply. The Incan civilization collapsed soon after the arrival of Europeans in the western hemisphere. Much of the rich culture of the Incas was lost.   J.M.C./S.O.

INCANDESCENCE (in′ kən des′ əns) Incandescence is the emission of visible light by any object at high temperature. An object at low temperature radiates infrared light, which is not visible to the human eye. (*See* SPECTRUM.) An object being heated starts to become incandescent when it gives off red light. Other colors are emitted until only white light is given off. The color is a good indication of the temperature. Red light indicates a lower temperature than white light.

Most artificial lighting in homes and offices is incandescent. In 1880, the first electric light bulbs using the principle of incandescence were produced. *See also* LUMINESCENCE.   J.M.C./J.T.

INCENSE CEDAR (in' sens' sēd' ər) The incense cedar is a tree that is not a cedar but a member of the cypress family. It grows to heights greater than 30 m [100 ft]. It has dark green leaves that grow in overlapping groups of four pairs. The cones are less than 2.5 cm [1 in] long, and have six scales. Four of the scales carry one or two winged seeds.

Incense cedars grow in California and Oregon. Its fragrant wood is used in carpentry. J.M.C./M.H.S.

INDIAN CIVILIZATION (in' dē ən siv' ə lə zā' shən) The Indians of the Western Hemisphere are the true native Americans. Christopher Columbus named them ''Indians'' when he arrived in the New World because he thought he had reached India.

The ancestors of the Indians probably came to the Americas during the ice age. At that time, the ocean level dropped because of glaciation, exposing land that is now underwater. The Indians' ancestors probably crossed a land bridge from Asia, where the Bering Strait is now. From there, the Indians moved southward throughout North and South America. When the Europeans arrived in the New World, most of the Indians lived in small villages and subsisted by hunting and fishing. The major Indian political states were, however, limited to Central and South America. These areas still have a large Indian population. Many of them have intermarried with Europeans and some with Africans.

The situation in North America was quite different. Most Indians had their land taken away by the white settlers. The Indians were continually pushed further west as the white settlements expanded. Today, many North American Indians still live on reservations, although increasing numbers live off reservations in urban centers and elsewhere.

Contributions of the Indians The Indians made countless contributions to the society of the United States. Many Indian words are used to describe places and things. More than half of the states' names are Indian words, such as Connecticut, Massachusetts, and Illinois. Many names of American cities, like Miami and Cheyenne, are Indian words.

The Indians introduced Europeans to new foods such as corn, avocados, cacao, peanuts, peppers, potatoes, pumpkins, and tomatoes. The Indians also cultivated tobacco.

Indians developed a number of kinds of canoes, which were their most common means of water travel. There were large dugout canoes, bark canoes, and light boats made of reeds. The Indians of the north were the first people to use toboggans and snowshoes. Indians also played games that have since evolved into lacrosse and field hockey.

The Indians made important contributions to the field of medicine. The Incas used cocaine, derived from the coca plant, for medicinal purposes. Other tribes used quinine to fight malaria and curare to fight tetanus. *See also* INCAN CIVILIZATION; MAYAN CIVILIZATION. J.M.C./S.O.

INDICATOR (in' də kāt' ər) Indicators are substances that are used by chemists to show when a chemical reaction has finished. The most common use for indicators is in reactions between acids and bases. (*See* ACID; BASE.) Acids and bases react together to form a salt and water. They are said to neutralize each other. The strength of an acid or a base is measured by its pH. (*See* PH.) Water has a pH of 7. An acid has a pH of less than 7. The more acidic the solution, the lower the pH. Bases have a pH of between 7 and 14. The stronger the base, the higher the pH.

The most common kind of indicator is a dye that changes color over a range of pH. An example is a purple dye called litmus. (*See* LITMUS.) Litmus is red in an acidic solution and blue in a basic solution. Suppose that a few drops of litmus are added to a base. An acidic solution is slowly added. When enough acid has been added, the solution turns pink

Name of Indicator		
METHYL ORANGE		
METHYL RED		
METHYL VIOLET		
BROMOTHYMOL BLUE		
THYMOL BLUE		
PHENOLPHTHALEIN		

A table of some indicators used in chemical analysis, shows the pH range (degree of acidity) at which they change color.

because of the litmus. All indicators react with the compounds being tested. Litmus reacts with a base to form a blue dye and with acid to form a red dye. When the acid is added to the base, they immediately react together. Eventually the base is neutralized by the acid. When a little extra acid is added, it reacts with the litmus. Therefore the color of the solution changes from blue to red.

Indicators are frequently used to find out the strength of a solution. Suppose that the acid solution has a certain, known strength. The volume of acid added can be measured and so can the volume of the basic solution. Then the strength of the base can be calculated. Litmus changes color over a wide range of pH and so is only suitable for strong acids and bases. Other indicators are more accurate since they change color over a smaller range. A universal indicator is a mixture of different indicators. Its color changes throughout the pH scale. It is used to make a quick and rough guess of the pH of a solution. A different kind of indicator is the precipitation indicator. Precipitation is when a chemical reaction causes a solid to form quickly in a reaction. *(See* PRECIPITATION.) Precipitation indicators produce a precipitation when the reaction is completed.

Indicators are also used in oxidation-reduction reactions. *(See* OXIDATION AND RE-DUCTION.) They are called oxidation-reduction indicators, or redox indicators. They work in the same way. The indicator is one color when it is oxidized and a different color when it is reduced. M.E./A.D.

INDIGO (in′ di gō′) Indigo is a deep blue dye used to color cotton and wool. The pigment in indigo is called indigotin. This dye was once obtained from several plants, especially the indigo plant. The indigo plant, which grows chiefly in India, is a member of the pea family. Indigo is now made artificially. Synthetic indigo is a dye called alizarin. *See also* DYE. J.J.A./J.D.

INDIUM (in′ dē əm) Indium (In) is a very soft, silvery white metallic element. The atomic number of indium is 49 and its atomic weight is 114.82. Its melting point is 156.6°C [313.9°F] and it boils at 2,080°C [3776°F]. Its relative density is 7.3. It was discovered in 1863 by the German chemists Ferdinand Reich and Hieronymus Richter. Indium is a rare element and occurs mainly in zinc minerals. Indium compounds have a deep indigo blue color in a flame. That is why the metal is called indium.

Indium is used to make alloys that have low melting points. These alloys are used in soldering and in fire alarm systems. It is also used in electronic components such as transistors and in making mirrors. M.E./J.R.W.

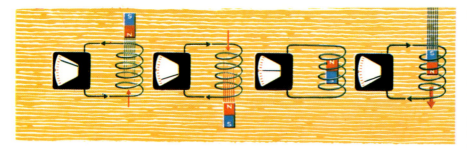

Electromagnetic induction is shown at left. 1. Moving a magnet through a coil induces a current in the coil. 2. Moving the magnet the other way reverses the current. 3. If the magnet stops moving, the voltage is zero. 4. If the magnet moves faster, it induces a higher voltage.

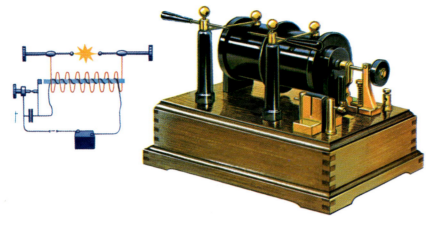

An induction coil and circuit diagram (far left) are shown. Low voltage current passing through the primary (inside) coil is rapidly switched on and off, alternatively magnetizing and demagnetizing the iron core. This induces a high voltage "kick" in the secondary (outside) coil, causing a spark to jump across the spark gap. A transformer is shown at left.

INDUCTION (in dək′ shən) Electromagnetic induction was first discovered by an English scientist, Michael Faraday. (*See* FARADAY, MICHAEL.) He placed some wire between the poles of a magnet. Then he joined the ends of the wire through an instrument that could detect an electric current. When the wire was moved through the magnetic field, a current flowed through it. This is called electromagnetic induction.

Faraday also discovered a similar effect. He placed two coils of wire near to each other. Then he passed an alternating current through one of the coils. An alternating current is continually changing and reverses its flow at short intervals. Because the current is changing, it sets up a magnetic field around itself. This field changes with the current. Faraday found that a similar current is induced in the second coil. It is induced by the changing magnetic field.

This effect is used in transformers. (*See* TRANSFORMER.) They are used to change high voltages to low ones, and vice versa. In a transformer, the voltage in one coil is used to induce a voltage in the other. The size of the induced voltage depends on the number of turns of wire in each coil. *See also* ELECTROMAGNETISM.　M.E./J.T.

INDUCTION (LOGICAL) Induction (in dək′ shən) is a method of investigation used by scientists. When scientists perform experiments, they make observations. They then try to explain the results of their observations in a theory. Then they, or other scientists, perform more experiments to test the theory. This method of investigating the world is called induction. It is the opposite of deduction. In deduction, you start with a theory. Then you perform experiments to confirm that the theory is accurate. *See also* SCIENCE.　M.E./A.I.

INERTIA (in ər′ shə) Inertia is the tendency of matter to remain at rest unless acted upon by an outside force. Inertia is also the tendency of a moving body to continue moving in the same direction. The greater the mass of the matter, the greater its inertia. For example, an automobile has greater inertia than a bicycle. It takes less effort to get the bicycle moving than it does to get the automobile moving. A person sitting in a moving automobile that stops suddenly still keeps moving forward unless stopped by a safety belt.

W.R.P./J.T.

INERTIAL GUIDANCE (in ər′ shəl gīd′ əns) Inertial guidance is a system of navigating that does not depend upon observations of stars, planets, or the sun. Its function depends only on measurements of amount and direction of accelerations, or changes in velocity. It is used mainly in nuclear submarines, missiles, rockets, and transoceanic air transport planes.

Nuclear submarines are able to remain submerged for many months without surfacing. By remaining submerged, they reduce the risk of detection. However, they are not able to navigate by conventional methods. A special computer in the inertial guidance system records every change in the ship's speed and direction, the speed of currents under the ocean, and other factors. The computer can determine instantly the exact location of the submarine. Direction-sensing instruments that contain gyroscopes and speed-detecting devices, called accelerometers, feed information to the computer.

Most missiles and rockets employ a modified version of the submarine inertial guidance system. This system keeps the missile, or rocket, on a pre-selected course, and automatically makes corrections when it wanders from the desired path. W.R.P./J.vP.

INFECTION (in fek′ shən) Infection is the invasion of the body by any germs causing disease, such as bacteria, viruses, or other microorganisms. The body has defenses against infection. The secretion of its glands helps to control bacteria. The skin forms a strong barrier. Most body openings, such as the ears, nose, and mouth, are lined with membranes that secrete sticky mucus to trap germs. Within the body there is a powerful system that attacks invading germs and neutralizes (makes harmless) their poisons. (*See* IMMUNITY.)

Germs can enter the body through breaks in the skin caused by injury or surgery. This is why cuts and burns must be kept clean. It is also why surgeons must make sure that their hands, clothes, and instruments are completely germ-free. (*See* ASEPSIS.) Biting insects spread a number of diseases by piercing the skin of their victims. Some germs can pass through the mucous membranes.

Many germs infect the body through the stomach and intestines. Such infection may result if a person consumes contaminated food or water. Many common germs are, however, destroyed by the acid in the stomach. The easiest route of all for many germs is by way of the lungs. A large number of common infectious diseases are spread by people breathing in tiny droplets of germ-filled moisture. These droplets are sprayed into the air whenever a person with an infectious disease coughs, sneezes, or simply exhales.

The use of antiseptics and other hygienic measures can reduce the chance of infection. (*See* HYGIENE.) But some diseases are so infectious that patients must be kept in isolation, or out of contact with other people except medical staff who are immune or specially protected. J.J.A./J.J.F.

INFINITY (in fin′ ət ē) Infinity means an unlimited extent of space, time, or quantity. If you start counting the whole numbers from one, you will never reach the end. There is always a number bigger than any number that you can think of. The whole numbers are said to reach infinity. This simply means that they go on "forever." Infinity is sometimes represented by the symbol ∞. M.E./S.P.A.

Facing left: the inflorescence of the hollyhock.

INFLAMMATION (in' flə mā' shən)

Inflammation is a way in which the body reacts to injury or infection. The infected tissues become swollen, reddened, and warm. The inflamed area feels painful. The body temperature and pulse rate may both be increased. These changes are a result of the blood vessels in the area becoming dilated (enlarged), increasing the blood flow. The blood cells and blood vessels press on sensory nerves, causing pain. The walls of the capillaries, the smallest blood vessels, become more porous (filled with tiny holes). This allows white blood cells and other things in the blood to pass out to the affected tissues and to help to repair them or kill germs. J.J.A./J.J.F.

INFLORESCENCE (in' flə res' əns)

An inflorescence is a cluster of flowers. Single flowers, such as the tulip, and flowers that grow at the bases of leaves, such as the morning glory, are not considered to be inflorescences. There are two basic types of inflorescence: determinate inflorescence and indeterminate inflorescence. In determinate inflorescence, the stem stops growing when a flower develops from a bud at the tip of the stem. (*See* HORMONE.) In determinate inflorescence, the stem continues growing as flowers develop near the tip. As the stem grows, more flowers are produced. As a result, the lower or inner flowers are older than the upper or outer ones. A.J.C./M.H.S.

INFLUENZA (in' flü en' zə)

Influenza is a disease caused by several different kinds of viruses. It is a very infectious disease. It spreads very rapidly from person to person. When a large number of people in the same area are affected, it is called an epidemic of influenza.

The influenza virus settles in the lining of the nose and throat. It causes sneezing, coughing, and sore throat. It can cause fever, sudden chills, and headache. Often the sufferer has aches and pains all over the body. He or she feels sick and completely exhausted. In most cases, influenza lasts between three days and a week.

Some kinds of influenza are very mild. Others are dangerous. The "Spanish flu" epidemic after World War I killed more people than were killed in the war itself. Fortunately there have been no more influenza epidemics as serious as that. However, because people can travel long distances very

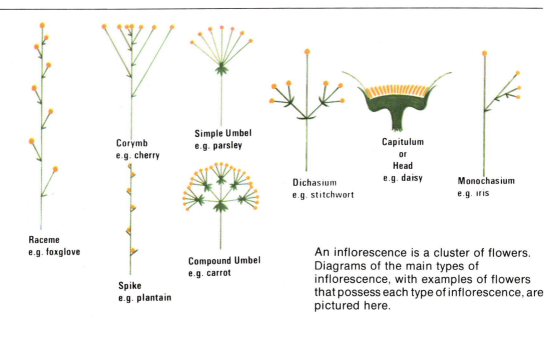

Raceme
e.g. foxglove

Corymb
e.g. cherry

Simple Umbel
e.g. parsley

Spike
e.g. plantain

Compound Umbel
e.g. carrot

Dichasium
e.g. stitchwort

Capitulum
or
Head
e.g. daisy

Monochasium
e.g. iris

An inflorescence is a cluster of flowers. Diagrams of the main types of inflorescence, with examples of flowers that possess each type of inflorescence, are pictured here.

rapidly today, epidemics may spread quickly around the world.

It is possible to prepare vaccines that give protection against virus diseases. But there are so many different kinds of influenza that it is hard to prepare vaccines against them. If there seems to be a danger of an epidemic, then a vaccine against a particular kind of influenza can be prepared. The exact type of virus responsible is first identified. Millions of doses must be prepared to give the population immunity against the disease. (*See* IMMUNITY.) D.M.H.W./J.J.F.

INFRARED RAY (in′ frə red′ rā′) An infrared ray is a beam of light that has a longer wavelength than visible light, and therefore cannot be seen by the human eye. Infrared rays are part of the electromagnetic spectrum. All objects give off infrared rays according to their temperature. The warmer an object is, the more infrared rays it gives off. During World War II, an instrument called a sniperscope was used to detect something warmer than its surroundings. This was valuable in finding enemies hiding in the dark or in fog. Infrared rays also have applications in photography and medical treatment. (*See* MEDICINE.)

Infrared rays were discovered by the British astronomer Sir William Herschel in 1800. J.M.C./S.S.B.

INFRASONICS (in′ frə sän′ iks) Infrasonics is the study of vibrations, similar to sound waves, that have a very low frequency. Infrasonic waves are so low in frequency that they cannot be heard. They are below 20 hertz, which is the lowest frequency the human ear can hear. However, infrasonic waves can be felt, and, if the intensity, or strength, is high the vibrations can be damaging to the body tissue. *See also* FREQUENCY; SOUND. W.R.P./J.T.

INGOT (ing′ gət) An ingot is a mass of metal cast into a size or shape convenient for storing, reshaping, or refining. For example, a gold ingot is often shaped like a bar. Steel ingots range in weight from a few grams or ounces to many tons. In addition to gold and steel, silver and tin are often cast into ingots. J.M.C./R.W.L.

INJECTION (in jek′ shən) In medicine, many drugs or other fluids are forced into an opening, passage, or tissue in the body. The fluid enters the body through a hollow needle

This infrared photograph of the Rio Grande river was taken from a mile above the Texas-Mexico border. The pale blue of the river (left, above silvery patch of reflected sunlight) shows the presence of silt caused by pollution. The contrasting tones of the oxbow lake (top center) and the lagoon (upper right) are the result of variations in the amount of infrared light reflected—again suggesting water pollution by different substances.

that penetrates the skin. This process is called injection. Injection may be performed in a number of ways.

The equipment needed to perform a hypodermic injection includes a syringe and a hollow needle. A syringe is a tube attached to a plunger. The needle has a very sharp point. It slips easily into the skin. The doctor attaches the needle to the syringe barrel. He puts the liquid medicine in the syringe and places the needle into the patient's skin. The doctor then presses on the plunger. This forces the medicine through the needle. There are different types of hypodermic injections. They are named for the tissue into which the injection is made. Intradermal injections are made between the layers of skin. Injections made below the layers of skin are called subcutaneous injections. In an intramuscular injection, the needle penetrates a muscle.

A hypodermic needle can be used to give an intravenous injection. An intravenous injection is one given inside a vein. Doctors use intravenous injections to put needed substances into the bloodstream. When blood, blood plasma, or serum is given this way, it is called a transfusion. Patients who cannot eat or drink are kept alive by intravenous feeding of water containing sugar, amino acids, vitamins, and minerals. *See also* BLOOD TRANSFUSION. J.J.A./J.J.F.

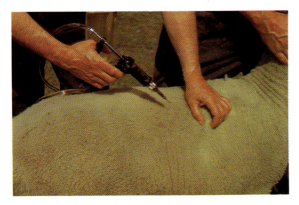

A sheep is being given an injection.

INORGANIC CHEMISTRY (in′ ȯr′ gan′ ik kem′ ə strē) Chemistry is the study of elements and compounds. Compounds are formed when different elements combine with each other. Compounds are divided into two groups: organic compounds and inorganic compounds. Inorganic chemistry studies the chemical properties of inorganic compounds. It also studies the chemical properties of the elements themselves. Roughly speaking, inorganic compounds do not contain carbon. However a few carbon compounds are counted as inorganic, such as the gas carbon dioxide. People used to think that organic compounds only occurred in living, or organic, matter. Inorganic compounds were thought to be found only in minerals and nonliving, or inorganic, matter. But this is now known to be not strictly true. M.E./A.D.

INSECT

An insect (in′ sekt) is any of more than one million species of invertebrate animals belonging to the class Insecta of the phylum Arthropoda. (*see* ARTHROPODA.) Insects live almost everywhere in the world except in the deep seas. They are the most widespread and successful animals that ever lived. Fossils indicate that insects existed more than 400 million years ago. Since that time, they have consistently been able to adapt quickly and efficiently to changes in the climate and environment. (*See* ADAPTATION.)

Insect body The body of an insect is divided into three sections: head, thorax, and abdomen. The head has one pair of antennae that is used for the senses of touch, taste, and smell. There are usually two compound eyes which provide good vision, and two or three simple eyes (ocelli) which detect light or darkness. (*See* EYE AND VISION.) The mouth may have biting or chewing jaws, or may have piercing and sucking structures. The mouths of some insects have unmovable jaws with spongelike pads for absorbing liquids. The head also contains a brain which connects with nerve cords in all parts of the body.

The thorax, or middle part of the body, has three pairs of jointed legs. These legs are equipped with sticky pads or claws at the ends. Insects are the only invertebrates with wings. Although most insects have two pairs of wings, some have only one pair, or no wings at all. Some of the wingless insects have small knobs where the wings would normally be. (*See* VESTIGIAL ORGAN.) Other wingless insects may have lost the wings during evolution or may never have had wings at any point in their history. (*See* EVOLUTION.)

The abdomen, or end part of the body, contains organs for digestion, excretion, respiration, and reproduction. There are tiny openings along the length of the abdomen called spiracles. These spiracles open to the tracheae, or air tubes, through which an insect breathes. Oxygen diffuses into the blood from the tracheae at a fairly slow rate. (*See* DIFFUSION.) This is probably a major reason that insects have stayed small throughout evolution. The abdomen also contains malpighian tubules. (*See* EXCRETION.) These tubules remove wastes from the blood while recycling most of the water to the body. For this reason, insects can live for long periods of time without water. A female insect often has an egg-laying tube called an ovipositor. In some insects, the ovipositor has been modified for use as a stinger.

An insect's body is covered with a tough exoskeleton. (*See* SKELETON.) This exoskeleton is lighter and stronger than bone. It provides protection from injury and loss of moisture, and serves as a place of attachment for muscles. Since the exoskeleton does not in-

The goliath beetle (below) of Africa is the world's largest insect. It is about the size of an adult person's fist. Insects live almost everywhere in the world except in the deep seas. Insects existed more than 400 million years ago.

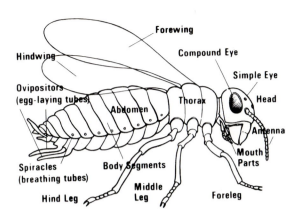

Forewing
Compound Eye
Hindwing
Simple Eye
Ovipositors (egg-laying tubes)
Thorax
Head
Abdomen
Antenna
Mouth Parts
Spiracles (breathing tubes)
Body Segments
Hind Leg
Middle Leg
Foreleg

The body of a typical adult insect (left) is divided into head, thorax, and abdomen, and covered with hard, horny chitin. Most insects have wings, and all have three pairs of legs. The head includes the brain, simple and compound eyes, antennae and mouth parts. Legs and wings are attached to the thorax. The abdomen contains the digestive, excretory, and reproductive organs.

Insects (below) are divided into three broad groups according to the extent of metamorphosis they undergo during their development into adults. The three groups are complete, incomplete, and gradual metamorphosis.

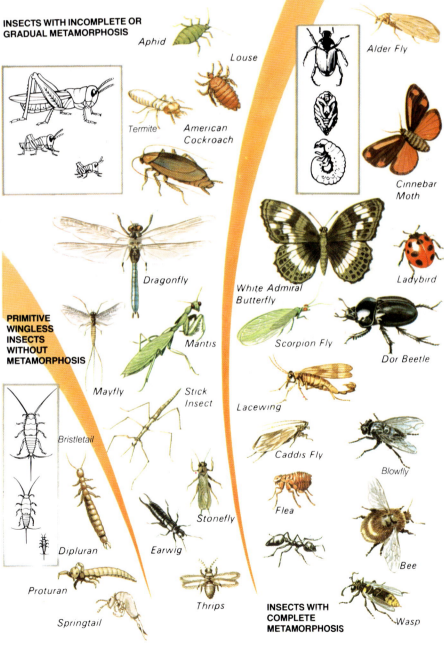

INSECTS WITH INCOMPLETE OR GRADUAL METAMORPHOSIS

Aphid

Louse

Alder Fly

Termite

American Cockroach

Cinnebar Moth

Dragonfly

White Admiral Butterfly

Ladybird

PRIMITIVE WINGLESS INSECTS WITHOUT METAMORPHOSIS

Mantis

Scorpion Fly

Dor Beetle

Mayfly

Stick Insect

Lacewing

Bristletail

Caddis Fly

Blowfly

Flea

Dipluran

Earwig

Stonefly

Bee

Proturan

Thrips

Wasp

Springtail

INSECTS WITH COMPLETE METAMORPHOSIS

crease in size as the insect grows larger, it must be shed several times during an insect's development. (*See* MOLTING.)

The entire body of an insect is usually covered with tiny bristles. These bristles are connected to nerves and are very sensitive to contact. It is for this reason that an insect can detect even the faintest breeze or movement.

Many insects have special hearing organs located on the abdomen, thorax, or legs. Some of these organs are spaces covered by a thin membrane which responds to vibrations in the air.

Insect life   One reason for the amazing success of insects is that they are able to reproduce quickly and in large numbers. Reproduction is usually sexual, the male inserting sperm into the female's body. As the female lays her eggs, they are fertilized by the sperm. (*See* FERTILIZATION.) The fertilized eggs are usually not tended by the insect, but develop near or in a source of nourishment and protection. In some cases, fertilization is external. This means that the female lays the eggs and then the male fertilizes them. Some insects produce eggs which develop into adults without being fertilized. (*See* PARTHE-NOGENESIS.)

As an insect develops, it goes through several changes before becoming an adult. Some primitive insects develop directly from the eggs. Most, however, go through several stages of development called metamorphosis. (*See* MEATMORPHOSIS.) In complete metamorphosis, there are four stages of development: egg, larva, pupa, adult. In incomplete metamorphosis, there are three stages: egg, nymph, adult. The nymph is like a small adult. As the insect goes through its development, it molts several times. The entire process of metamorphosis may take a few days or several years, depending on species and environmental conditions. Many insects lay eggs which can survive the winter or other unfavorable conditions. (*See* DORMANCY.)

Insects and human beings   Although many people think of insects as bothersome pests, most insects perform many important services. Harmful insects, however, cause losses of more than six billion dollars a year to crops and plants. Some insects bite or sting animals and human beings. Some of these biting insects carry disease-causing micro-organisms such as bacteria, fungi, viruses, and wormlike parasites. (*See* DISEASE; MICRO-ORGANISM.)

Many insects, however, are of vital importance to human beings. They are responsible for most of the pollination of plants. (*See* POLLINATION.) Some insects eat or live off of weeds or other, more harmful insects. Some insects make tunnels in the ground which help aerate the soil. Insects are the major source of food for birds, fish, and many other animals. In some countries, insects are used as food for human beings. Some insects feed on dead and decaying material, and form a vital link in the food chain. (*See* FOOD CHAIN.) Insects also provide silk, honey, and wax. Insects themselves are used as a source of substances used in dyes, shellacs, medicines, and many other products.

Insect control   Harmful insects are often controlled by chemicals called insecticides. (*See* INSECTICIDE.) Because of the ability of insects to adapt quickly to negative environmental conditions (such as being sprayed with insecticides), they soon become resistant to these chemicals. As a result, entomologists and other biologists are constantly experimenting with new, safer means of control. They have developed methods of introducing predators, parasites, and insect diseases to control insects. (*See* BIOLOGICAL CONTROL.) Recently, sterilized males have been used as a method of control. Large numbers of these males are released in areas where control is desired. They mate with the females which then lay unfertilized eggs. These eggs fail to develop. Since many harmful insects thrive in organic wastes, they can often be controlled by improving sanitary conditions. *See also* ENTOMOLOGY; PROTECTIVE COLORATION; WARNING COLORATION. A.J.C./J.E.R.

INSECTICIDE (in sek′ tə sīd′) An insecticide is a chemical used to kill insect pests. The use of insecticides has helped save many crops and ornamental plants that would have been killed by insects. The discovery of a very powerful insecticide called DDT (which stands for its chemical name of DichloroDiphenyl-Trichloroethane) was a major factor in winning battles in the South Pacific during World War II. The DDT was sprayed over islands where malaria-carrying mosquitoes lived. The malaria disease had killed and weakened many soldiers, but the soldiers were able to stay healthy after they killed the mosquitoes with DDT. (*See* MALARIA; MOSQUITO.)

There are some insecticides which are simple compounds found in nature. Most, however, are complex chemicals made by man. They kill insects in one of two ways. Some will kill the insect if it is sprayed on the body of the insect. Other insecticides have to be eaten in order to work. These are sprayed on leaves which insects eat.

Insecticides have caused problems, too. Many are poisonous to valuable animals such as birds and fish. When a large forest is sprayed with an insecticide, much of it will be washed by rains into the streams in the forest. In this way, fish can become poisoned. Often, animals such as worms will be sprayed by an insecticide. This will not kill the worm, but when a bird, such as a robin, eats several of these worms, it may die. Scientists have found that some birds of prey, such as ospreys and falcons, can survive with large amounts of insecticides in their bodies. However, this causes the shells of their eggs to be very thin and easy to break. Most eggs then break and few young birds are hatched. Because of this, ospreys and falcons are becoming very rare.

Another problem with many insecticides, such as DDT, is that they do not go away. When DDT is washed into a stream, it may stay in the mud or water for ten years. Because of this, many insecticides are no longer used in many countries.

In recent years, some insects—especially mosquitoes—have become immune to insecticides. The chemicals no longer kill them. (*See* IMMUNITY.) Scientists now understand why this happens. There are always a few mosquitoes that are not affected by a chemical. There may be only 2 out of 10,000 mosquitoes which survive a spraying of DDT. These two mosquitoes reproduce and their offspring inherit the immunity to DDT. (*See* GENETICS.) Soon there are 1,000 mosquitoes that are immune to DDT. In a few years, there are 10,000 mosquitoes again, but they are all immune to DDT. Scientists must keep developing new insecticides to kill these insects. *See also* AGRICULTURE; CONSERVATION, ECOLOGY. S.R.G./R.J.B.

An insecticide comes from the pyrethrum flower.

INSECTIVORE (in sek′ tə vôr′) An insectivore is an organism that eats insects. Most insectivores are animals, but there are insectivorous plants such as the Venus's-flytrap. Insects that land or crawl onto a special leaf of the plant are trapped and digested. Insectivorous animals include shrews, moles, bats, and other mammals. Some of them eat nothing but insects, but others also eat small animals such as worms. Insectivores usually have sharp teeth in order to kill and chew the insects, which sometimes have tough shells. *See also* CARNIVORE; HERBIVORE; OMNIVORE; VENUS'S-FLYTRAP.   S.R.G./R.J.B.

The common shrew (above) is a typical insectivore. Insectivores are organisms that eat insects.

INSOLATION (in′ sō lā′ shen) Insolation is the heat and light energy that the earth and other planets of the solar system receive from the sun. The word "insolation" comes from the three words "incoming solar radiation."

On earth, the greatest insolation is at the equator. The least insolation is at the North and South Poles. The amount of insolation depends upon the angle of the sun's rays. There is more insolation where the rays fall more directly. More solar radiation is received during the spring and summer than in the fall and winter. Insolation is not as great when the skies are cloudy or when there is a high pollution level in the atmosphere. *See also* CLIMATE; SEASON.   J.M.C./C.R.

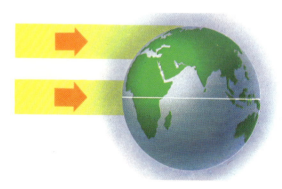

The earth's isolation is greatest at the equator and least at high altitudes.

The jaw fish (above) carries its eggs in its mouth to protect them—an example of parental instinct.

INSTINCT (in′ stingkt′) Instinct is a word that is used with different meanings in biology, psychology, and psychoanalysis.

In biology, instincts are inborn behavior patterns. The behavior is inherited rather than learned. Scientists use the terms instinct and instinctive behavior only for activity that involves neither experience nor learning. Examples of instinctive behavior are the maternal behavior of a mother towards her young, the reverse response in which the young follow their mother, the courtship behavior between male and female, and migration. In-

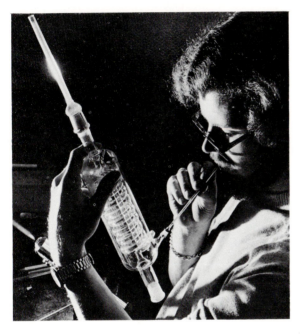

A thermograph (top left) records continuous temperature measurements. Traditional skills (bottom left) are used in making this glass condenser. An electron microscope (above) provides more powerful magnifications than optical microscopes.

stinctive behavior begins with a special stimulus, something that makes the animal act as it does.

In psychology, instincts are thought of as inborn biological impulses. These impulses drive the organism toward certain ends. In this sense, instincts are agents acting for creative, intellectual activities as well as for the preservation of the individual.

In psychoanalysis, instincts comprise the energy that causes tension and that drives the organism into action. *See also* BEHAVIOR OF ANIMALS; PSYCHOLOGY.   J.J.A./R.J.B.

INSTRUMENT, SCIENTIFIC A scientific instrument (in′ strə mənt) is a tool that people use to gather knowledge about the world around them. Everything that people know about their surroundings comes through their senses, such as sight, hearing, and smell. However, peoples' senses have limitations. That's where scientific instruments come into use. Some things are too small to see with the unaided eye. Other things are too far away. Some sounds are beyond the range of a person's hearing. Such things as electricity and atomic radiation can only be detected or measured by instruments.

People's senses do not provide precise enough information under all conditions. For example, our eyes can easily compare the brightness of two electric lights. But they are less effective at judging how bright one lighted room is compared to another. Sometimes, peoples' senses give misleading information. If you place one hand in cold water, and the other hand in hot water, both hands soon feel neither hot nor cold. If you then put both hands in lukewarm water, the hand that was in the hot water feels cool, and the other hand feels warm. Thermometers give you a much more accurate measurement of temperature than your hands.

Most scientific instruments have three things in common: (1) a transducer, (2) a scale of values, and (3) a readout. The transducer tells the quantity being measured. The scale of values provides a comparison with the output of the transducer. The readout gives the result of the instrument reading. A thermometer, for example, uses a glass tube containing mercury as a transducer. The numbers along the tube are the scale of values. The position of the mercury along the numbers provides the readout that tells what the temperature is.

There are two main types of scientific instruments—graphic instruments and measuring instruments. Graphic instruments present an entire picture at once so that one part of the picture can be compared to other parts. Cameras, microscopes, and telescopes are the best-known graphic instruments. Others include spectroscopes, oscilloscopes, and nuclear particle detectors. (*See* ACCELERATOR, PARTICLE.)

Measuring instruments tell the number of measurement units involved in whatever they are measuring. A measuring stick tells the length of a table in meters and centimeters, or feet and inches. A micrometer can measure the thickness of such materials as paper, or thin metal foil. The laser rangefinder can measure the distance from the earth to the moon within centimeters.

Accurate measurement plays such an important part in science that some people believe science is basically measurement. Quantities most often measured include length, temperature, electric current, time, and weight. Most other measured quantities are related to these basic ones. Each kind of quantity requires a certain kind of measuring in-

strument to measure it. Many types of thermometers measure temperature. Balances and scales measure weight. Clocks measure time. Several types of instruments, including ammeters and voltmeters, measure electricity. W.R.P./R.W.L.

INSULATION (in′ sə lā′ shən) Insulation is material that protects against heat, cold, electricity, or sound. Clothing is one of the most common types of insulation. Wool clothes are warmer than those made of most other fabrics. Air becomes trapped in the meshes of the wool fiber. This dead (motionless) air does not conduct heat easily, and serves as a protective layer between the body and the outside air. This prevents body heat from escaping. Other kinds of insulation do not readily permit electricity or sound to pass through. These include the rubber or other coating that surrounds electrical wires, and the soundproofing found in theaters and homes.

Many materials provide protection against heat and cold. The body is protected by clothing made of various textiles. Generally, several layers of light clothing provide greater protection than one thick layer with the same total weight. This is due to the insulating effect of the air between the layers. The same principle is applied to insulation in homes and other structures. For example, the layer of air between storm windows and the regular windows provides insulation.

Home insulation is extremely important for comfortable and economical living. The loss of heat in uninsulated houses is so high that insulation in the outside walls and top ceilings pays for itself in lower fuel bills. The hollow spaces in walls and ceilings are usually filled with insulation. Several types of insulation are used for houses, including (1) batt, (2) blanket, (3) loose-fill, (4) rigid, and (5) reflective insulation.

Batt insulation is made in soft, flexible units that fit between rafters and joists. Batts are made of fireproof, fibrous material, such as treated wood fiber, hair felt, flax fiber, eel grass, or shredded paper. This material is stitched between two layers of waterproof paper. Batts are available in thicknesses up to 15 cm [6 in]. The fill material in batts may also be made of mineral wool, an insulating material made from the slag (mineral refuse) recovered from iron-making blast furnaces.

Blanket insulation is similar to batt insulation, but it comes in long rolls instead of pieces. A roll usually contains about 9 square meters [100 sq ft]. Loose-fill insulation comes in bulk form, in bags, or bales. Mineral wool in the form of pellets, expanded mica, granulated cork, and other materials are types of loose-fill insulation. Loose-fill insulation is poured or blown into place.

Rigid insulation consists of thick sheets of fiberboard. It is usually nailed to the outside walls, and then covered with wood siding or bricks. Reflective insulation consists of thin copper or aluminum sheets, or of copper or aluminum foil. It is often applied to the surfaces of rigid insulation, plasterboard, or even heavy paper. The metallic surfaces of these materials reflect heat waves.

Other kinds of heat and cold insulation include asbestos and cork. Both materials are expensive and have specialized uses. Asbestos is used to insulate furnaces and hot pipes. Cork is used in refrigeration.

Refractory materials are used to insulate against high temperatures in industrial furnaces, boilers, and incinerators. Refractories are made of non-metallic substances such as quartzite, sandstone, fire clay, bauxite, and graphite. They withstand temperatures of up to 1760°C [3200°F], well over the melting point of iron. Refractories also resist thermal shock (sudden large changes in temperature), and chemical actions of gases and liquids.

Soundproofing is a type of insulation. There are two different types. One type consists of sound-absorbing or sound-deadening, materials placed on walls and ceilings to reduce echoes. These materials make a speaker's voice more distinct. They also improve the quality of music by reducing objectionable echoes. Materials used for this purpose are perforated cardboard, fiberboard, corkboard, hair felt covered with burlap, and special types of acoustical tiles and plaster. These materials reduce echoes because they contain many air passages that take excess energy away from sound waves.

Another type of soundproofing reduces the sound transferred from room to room by vibration of the walls and floors. Sound waves make these surfaces vibrate. This causes air in contact with these surfaces to vibrate and cause other sounds. This type of sound transmission is difficult to overcome. However, building materials such as concrete, brick, and stone are used because they produce less vibration than wood and fiberboard. Floor coverings, such as carpets, heavy linoleum, rubber tiles, and cork tiles help insulate against floor vibrations. (*See* ACOUSTICS.)

Electrical insulation is made from materials that do not conduct electricity. These include rubber, glass, cotton, paraffin, certain plastics, and other materials.   W.R.P./J.T.

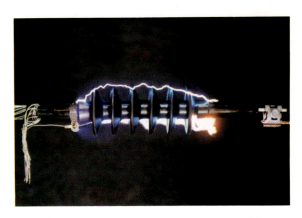

A terminal insulator (above) is being tested for a 15,000 volt power cable. Flashover for this insulator happens at over 165,000 volts—more than 10 times the voltage the insulator is supposed to absorb during normal use.

INSULIN (in' sə lən) Insulin is a chemical called a hormone that is produced in the body. (*See* HORMONE.) It is made in parts of the pancreas, a gland near the stomach. (*See* GLAND; PANCREAS.) When we eat sugary or starchy foods, these are broken down, or digested, in the body. They are digested into a simple sugar called glucose. Glucose passes into the bloodstream. When there is a lot of glucose in the blood, insulin pours from the pancreas into the bloodstream. Insulin helps the body use the glucose in the blood. The body uses glucose to provide energy for moving about and keeping warm. If not enough insulin is made in the pancreas, a person has the disease called sugar diabetes. (*See* DIABETES.) A person with diabetes is called a diabetic. Some diabetics are treated with repeated doses of insulin given by injection.　　　　　　　　　　　　D.M.H.W./J.J.F.

INTEGRATED CIRCUIT (int′ ə grāt′ əd sər′ ket) An ordinary electronic circuit consists of various components connected together by wires. An integrated circuit has all its components on one small piece of semiconductor. (*See* SEMICONDUCTOR.) Usu-

The integrated circuit (left) forms part of an electronic computer memory.

This listening device (below), which is clipped onto a necktie, has integrated circuits inside of it.

ally the semiconductor is a thin piece or wafer of silicon. Different amounts of impurities are added to different parts of the silicon. This makes the different parts behave like different components. For example, these parts may become resistors or diodes.

The first step in making an integrated circuit is to design a mask. The mask contains the pattern of the components that is to be placed on the wafer of silicon. Where a component is wanted, the mask is transparent. Otherwise it is dark. The pattern is then shrunk to the size of the wafer by using photography. The wafer of silicon is first coated with a layer of oxide. This protects the silicon. Then it is coated with a material that is sensitive to light. The mask is placed on the wafer and light is shown on it. The light only hits the wafer where a component is going to be. The light affects the light-sensitive layer. It can now be washed away. The oxide layer underneath is then removed by washing the wafer in acid. Then the impurities are passed into the wafer. They turn the silicon into a semiconductor. The exposed parts of the wafer have now become components.

Integrated circuits are very small. Usually they are about a thousandth of a centimeter [0.0004 in] thick. Their sides are about a tenth of a centimeter [0.04 in] across. Yet they can contain a hundred or more components. Very small but complicated equipment can be built with integrated circuits. They are used in pocket calculators. If ordinary circuits were used, the calculators would be many times larger.

M.E./L.L.R.

INTELLIGENCE (in tel′ ə jəns) Most scientists define intelligence as the ability to learn or understand. People differ in the speed in which they learn things. They differ in their ability to understand ideas. They differ in how well and how long they remember ideas. They also differ in how they use their knowledge and memory of situations in the past to solve problems. There is no fully ac-

cepted definition of intelligence. But intelligence involves the abilities mentioned above.

Such abilities are not separate things. They are all related. However, a person may do well in one thing and poorly in another. A person may find it very easy to memorize names and dates. But that person may find it difficult to do long division. Someone may have great creative talent in art or music, but can't remember where he or she left an object. Although creativity and intelligence are related, some people of above-average intelligence do poorly when faced with problems totally new to them.

Many psychologists believe that intelligence can be measured with various kinds of tests. These scientists believe that if a person can deal well with a problem in a test, that person can also deal with problems in everyday life. Psychologists figure the results of an intelligence test in a number called an IQ. IQ stands for intelligence quotient. To determine this number, they first give tests to find the person's mental age. Two children, one 8 years old and the other 16, may both have a mental age of 12. The younger child has certainly developed faster than the older one. But the mental age does not show the difference in the rates of mental growth. The mental age of the younger child is far above his chronological age (age in years). The older child's mental age is far below his or her chronological age. Therefore, psychologists have developed a formula:

$$IQ = \frac{MA \text{ (mental age)}}{CA \text{ (chronological age)}} \times 100$$

This means that the person's mental age is divided by his or her chronological age. The quotient is multiplied by 100. The resulting number is the IQ. This number stands for the way that someone's intelligence compares with that of other people the same age. The 8-year-old child's IQ is 150. The 16-year-old child's is 75.

Chimpanzees and humans are the two most intelligent animals. Facing left: a human infant and a chimpanzee infant. The chimpanzee and the human develop physical alertness and communication skills at different speeds.

Many people believe that intelligence tests do not really measure intelligence. Many tests seem to measure what someone has learned. They do not measure how quickly or slowly a person can learn. Therefore, these tests do not give a complete picture of the many factors that make up intelligence.

There is no absolute answer to where intelligence comes from. Scientists are still trying to find out what makes one person intelligent and another not so intelligent. But it can be said that peoples' intelligence depends on their heredity and their environment. Every person is born with a certain mental ability. The development of that ability may be activated or slowed down by his or her background. A child whose family speaks several languages, but depends on outside help for simple mechanical repairs, will probably find learning a new language easier than learning how an automobile engine works. A child who suffered from a very poor diet in infancy may not be able to develop his or her natural abilities. In a similar way, a child who was constantly ridiculed or beaten may become so upset that he or she may not be able to develop intellectual abilities. Many children who face discrimination because of race or physical defects fail to develop their mental abilities.

Generally, intelligence seems to be a result of both heredity and upbringing. Scientists have long disagreed about which is the more important. They will probably continue to do so for a long time. Despite major findings and advances in all fields of science, much about the human mind remains a mystery. *See also* BINET, ALFRED.   J.J.A./J.J.F.

INTENSITY (in ten′ sət ē) Intensity is the measure of the strength of radiant energy, such as light, magnetism, and sound.

Light intensity is the energy in watts sent out from a source over a given area. The area is usually a "solid angle" of a sphere called a steradian. (*See* LIGHT; PHOTOMETRY.)

The intensity of a magnetic field is measured in units of gauss. The intensity of the Earth's magnetic field is about 0.5 gauss. A magnetometer is the instrument used to measure the strength of a magnetic field. (*See* MAGNETISM.)

Sound intensity is measured in watts per square centimeter. When measuring the difference in intensity of two sounds, a unit called the bel is used. Each bel means an increase or decrease of 10 times the intensity. Therefore, if a fire engine siren has an intensity of ten times greater than the intensity of a buzzer, the siren has an intensity 1 bel greater than the buzzer. The decibel (1/10 of a bel) is the more common unit for measuring sound intensity. *See also* DECIBEL; SOUND.   J.M.C./J.T.

INTERFERENCE (int′ ə fir′ əns) All waves have crests (high points) and troughs (low points). A crest is where the disturbance is greatest in one direction. A trough is where the disturbance is greatest in the other direction. In a sea wave, for example, the highest point of the wave is the crest. The lowest point is the trough.

Interference is when two waves combine to reinforce or cancel each other out. The two waves must have about the same wavelength to interfere. The wavelength is the distance between one crest and the next. The waves must also be coherent. This means that the crests and troughs of different parts of the wave must coincide.

Interference can occur with any kind of wave, such as sound waves, water waves, light and radio waves. An easy way to produce interference is to pass a lightwave through two holes. This splits the wave up. After the two parts pass through the holes, they recombine and interfere. In some places, the crests of the two waves coincide. At these points, the light is strongest. This is called constructive interference. In other places, the crest of one wave coincides with the trough of the other. This is called destructive interference. The two waves cancel each other out. If light is used, then a series of light and dark bands are produced. This is called an interference pattern.

Interference can also occur between radio waves. The aerial of a radio receiver may pick up an unwanted signal. This signal can interfere with the main signal being picked up by the aerial. The interference produces a background crackling or hiss. Lightning causes interference with radio signals, as do some electric motors. A radio station sometimes broadcasts on a frequency close to that of another station. (*See* FREQUENCY.) These two signals can also interfere with one another.

M.E./A.I.

Two sets of water waves illustrate interference. If the crests of one set of waves meet the troughs of another, they cancel each other out and the waves disappear. If crests meet crests, they reinforce each other.

INTERFEROMETER (int′ ə fə räm′ ət ər) An interferometer is an instrument that produces interference of light. (*See* INTERFERENCE.) An American physicist, Albert Michelson, invented a very accurate interferometer around 1880. In the Michelson interferometer, a beam of light is first split by a special mirror. The mirror reflects some of the light and the rest passes through it. The two beams are then combined by other mirrors. The beams travel different distances and so are now out of step. Because they are out of

step, they interfere destructively. The interference pattern can be viewed. Interferometers are used to measure the wavelengths of light rays.

Interference can also be produced between two radio waves. This effect is used in radio astronomy. Two radio telescopes pick up signals from the same source. These two signals are then combined in an interferometer. Their interference pattern tells scientists more about the source than one signal would.

M.E./S.S.B.

INTERFERON (int′ ər fir′ än′) When viruses attack the body, it produces a substance called interferon. Interferon stops viruses from spreading and multiplying.

Viruses can multiply only by getting into a living cell. Viruses use the cell's own machinery to make new viruses. This usually kills the cell. The viruses then spread to nearby cells and repeat their work. Interferon is made whenever cells are attacked. In other words, the presence of a certain virus in a cell stimulates (causes) the cell to make interferon.

Interferon was discovered in 1957. It works only within a single species. For example, mouse interferon does not protect human beings. Human interferon does not help mice. Attempts to make interferon in a test tube have failed. But in 1970, scientists discovered that placing a form of nucleic acid made in the laboratory into animals causes their bodies to make interferon. When this is done, the creatures are much more able to fight off attack by viruses. Most scientists believe that the main use of interferon will be to prevent, rather than cure, disease. *See also* IMMUNITY.

J.J.A./J.J.F.

INTERNAL COMBUSTION ENGINE (in tərn′ əl kəm bəs′ chən en′ jən) In an internal combustion engine, fuel is burned inside a cylinder to give off energy. Combustion is another word for burning. The engines that drive most cars and trucks work by internal combustion. They include gasoline, diesel, and Wankel engines. (*See* ENGINE.) In an external combustion engine, fuel is burned outside the engine to give heat. Steam engines work by external combustion. (*See* STEAM ENGINE.)

The first internal combustion engine was made in about 1860. It was invented by Jean Joseph Etienne Lenoir, an engineer who lived in Belgium. It burned gas. After this, in 1876, came the engine invented by Count Nikolaus August Otto, an engineer in Germany. His was the first engine to work on a four-stroke cycle. This kind of engine is still used today.

The first gasoline-burning engines that worked well were made in 1885 by the automobile pioneers Karl Benz and Gottlieb Daimler. Twelve years later, another German engineer, Rudolf Diesel, invented the diesel engine. It burned oil as fuel. In both gasoline and diesel engines, fuel is burned inside a cylinder. But in a gasoline engine, a spark from a spark plug causes the burning. In a diesel engine, the fuel is burned by pressing air so tightly together that it heats up. This system is called compression ignition. *See also* GAS TURBINE; ENGINE.   D.M.H.W./J.T.

In this internal combustion engine cylinder (below), expanding gases formed by the explosion of fuel in the cylinder force the piston down.

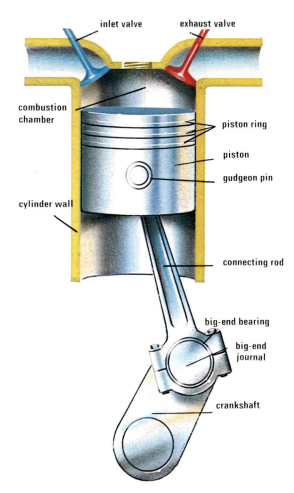

inlet valve
exhaust valve
combustion chamber
piston ring
piston
gudgeon pin
cylinder wall
connecting rod
big-end bearing
big-end journal
crankshaft

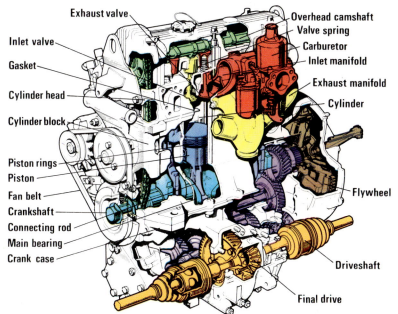

Exhaust valve
Inlet valve
Gasket
Cylinder head
Cylinder block
Piston rings
Piston
Fan belt
Crankshaft
Connecting rod
Main bearing
Crank case

Overhead camshaft
Valve spring
Carburetor
Inlet manifold
Exhaust manifold
Cylinder
Flywheel
Driveshaft
Final drive

- **Overhead camshaft**
- **Carburetor and gasoline intake**
- **Pistons**
- **Exhaust manifold and valve**
- **Crankshaft**
- **Clutch**
- **Gears**
- **Final drive and driveshaft**

A cutaway view of an overhead camshaft engine (left) is shown. Gasoline is mixed with air in the carburetor, the mixture enters the cylinders via the inlet manifold and inlet valves. The connecting rods turn the crankshaft, which operates the gears via the clutch. The gears turn the final drive, which is joined at the wheels by the driveshafts.

PROJECT SECTION

HELIOGRAPHY

Heliographs are signalling devices that use reflected sunlight. They provided rapid communication between towns in 11th century Algeria. In the 1800s, heliography became a popular means of communication between army units on the battlefield. Build the heliograph described below, and practice sending Morse code messages to your friends.

Procedure:

1. Glue wooden backing blocks to small mirrors. Screw them to brackets made by bending metal strips. One bracket should be about twice as long as the other.
2. Screw the brackets to a wooden baseboard. Screw two wooden strips to the front of the baseboard. These will support the shutter mechanism. (See diagram.)
3. Make the shutter mechanism from two pieces of thin wood. Cut three large identical slots in both pieces of wood. These slots should be the same size as the bars between the slots.
4. Make four small slots in one part of the shutter. This part will serve as the moving front of the mechanism. Pass wood screws through the slots. Screw them through the back of the shutter and into the two wooden strips. The screw heads must be a little larger than the width of the slots. The screws must be loose enough to allow the shutter front to slide smoothly up and down. Position the screws so that in the up position, the front of the shutter

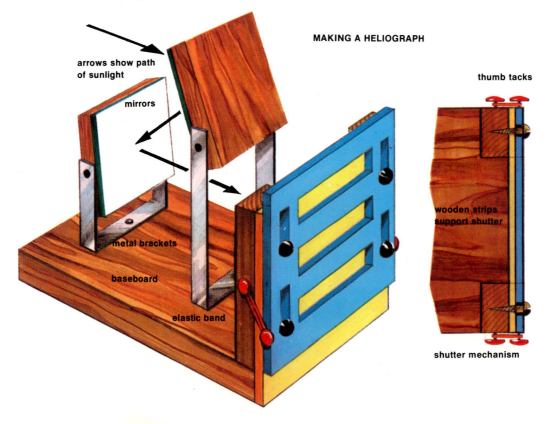

arrows show path of sunlight

mirrors

metal brackets

baseboard

elastic band

MAKING A HELIOGRAPH

thumb tacks

wooden strips support shutter

shutter mechanism

obscures the large slots behind. In the down position, these slots should be fully exposed.

5. Fasten four thumbtacks and two small elastic bands to the shutter mechanism. (See diagram.) With this arrangement, the shutter is normally held in the closed position.

Operation

Point the heliograph in the direction you wish to send signals. If sunlight is coming from the front, let it fall directly on the back mirror. In this case, the front mirror is not used. Adjust the angle of the back mirror so that sunlight is reflected onto the back of the shutter. Flashes of light can then be sent by pressing and releasing the shutter.

If the sun is behind you, arrange the mirrors so that light is reflected from the front mirror onto the back one. Then proceed as described above.

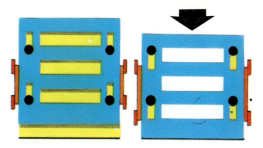

heliograph shutter closed (left), and open (right)

HUMIDITY

We often complain that a room feels uncomfortably hot or cold. But it is not always the room temperature that is too high or low. Air flow and humidity—the amount of moisture in the air—also affect our comfort. Build the hair hygrometer described below and use it to investigate how humidity variation affects your comfort.

Procedure:

1. Soak a hair in detergent and then rinse it in water to remove natural oils.
2. Nail one nail into each end of a square wood block about 7.5 cm by 10 cm [3 in by 4 in] wide.
3. Carefully tie one end of the hair to a rubber band. Twist the rubber band and attach it to one nail.
4. Attach a square piece of cardboard to one end of the block and glue a smaller block on the front of the larger one as shown in the diagram.

5. Pin a wooden cylinder between the small block and the cardboard.
6. Split the end of a drinking straw and glue it to the wooden cylinder as shown.
7. Wrap the hair once around the wooden cylinder and attach the other end to the other nail.
8. Mark a scale on the cardboard as shown.

Check to be sure that the hygrometer is working by placing it near a steaming kettle. The moisture should make the hair stretch and should cause the pointer to turn to the high end of the scale. The instrument will respond quite well to slow, day-to-day humidity changes. But it will take a long time to recover after being exposed to steam.

Adjust the position of the pointer by trial and error until, over long periods, its average position is at the center of the scale. You will then be able to see, at a glance, whether the humidity is above or below its normal level in your house.

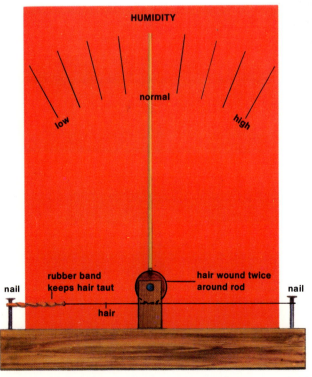

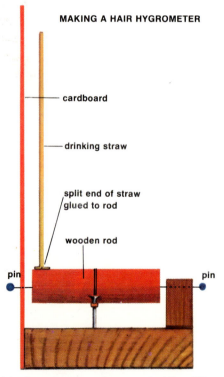

Two views of a hair hygrometer are shown above: left, a front view of a completed hair hygrometer; right, a side view showing placement of the different parts of the hair hygrometer.